Studies in Writing & Rhetoric

Other Books in the Studies in Writing & Rhetoric Series

Personally Speaking

Personally Speaking

Experience as Evidence in Academic Discourse

Candace Spigelman

SOUTHERN ILLINOIS UNIVERSITY PRESS

Carbondale

Publication partially funded by a subvention grant from The Conference on College
Composition and Communication of the National Council of Teachers of English.

Library of Congress Cataloging-in-Publication Data

Spigelman, Candace, [date]
    Personally speaking : experience as evidence in academic discourse / Candace
Spigelman.
        p. cm. — (Studies in writing & rhetoric)
    Includes bibliographical references (p.) and index.
    1. English language—Rhetoric—Study and teaching. 2. Autobiography—
Authorship—Study and teaching (Higher). 3. Academic writing—Study and
teaching. I. Title. II. Series.
PE1404.S747 2004
808'.042'0711—dc22   2004006879
ISBN 0-8093-2589-6 (cloth : alk. paper)
ISBN 0-8093-2590-X (pbk. : alk. paper)

Printed on recycled paper. ♻

The paper used in this publication meets the minimum requirements of American
National Standard for Information Sciences—Permanence of Paper for Printed
Library Materials, ANSI Z39.48-1992. ∞

For my parents, Dorothy and Fred Robinson
and for Michelle

We must attend, then, to the undemonstrated remarks and beliefs of experienced and older people or of intelligent people, no less than to demonstrations. For these people see correctly because experience has given them their eye.

—Aristotle, *Nicomachean Ethics*

One studies stories not because they are true or even because they are false, but for the same reason that people tell and listen to them, in order to learn about the terms on which others make sense of their lives.

—Linda Brodkey, "Writing Ethnographic Narratives"

Contents

Preface

Some years ago, when I first started teaching composition, a more experienced friend gave me this advice: "Never teach personal writing," he said. "Every student already has a bunch of stories to tell. They don't need more stories. They need writing that will serve." Although I appreciated my friend's admonition, then as now, I couldn't keep my students from writing the events of their lives into their papers. And I found that I enjoyed those nods toward experience, which often gave texture and detail to their essays. It's the same when I read published essays, including composition articles: examples drawn from a writer's life, especially a teaching life, have their own special appeal. Yet I understand why personal writing arouses concerns. If it doesn't "serve" our students' development as writers and as students, if it won't be accepted in other classes, if it's meant only as confession or disclosure, how can composition teachers justify or encourage such practice? Equally significant, if experiences are always filtered through the interpretive lenses of the writer, how can they be evidence? How can they be "true"?

In my own scholarly writing, I am sensitive to similar theoretical issues. Most of the time, I don't reveal my lived experiences or expose my personal life when I write composition articles or books. I stay away from such disclosures in part because I am a private person. Another reason is that while everyone may have a story, as my friend insisted, not everyone has stories she can use well. In fact, there are powerful and appropriate (and certainly inappropriate) ways to invoke our experiences, but if we want a stock of rhetorical advantages for ourselves and for our students, we'll need to understand *why* the personal can count as evidence and *how* to use it effectively.

The number of composition scholars who have begun to make arguments by way of personal narratives, anecdotes, and examples is expanding, and, in general, their arguments seem rhetorically appropriate. Moreover, consistent with contemporary autobiographical and essay theory, these arguments rarely fall prey to naive notions of the subject, nor do they appeal to foundational grounds of the "real." I don't think, however, that this increased acceptance of life writing foretells a broad-based move toward the personal in academic discourse. Nor do I think that allowance for the personal within scholarly genres will necessarily lead to the teaching of alternative discourses in composition classrooms. In both cases, I believe that for a more dramatic turn to occur, scholars and teachers must understand how the experiential example and narrative proof can function within academic arguments; they must also be able to evaluate arguments that invoke personal evidence.

In *Personally Speaking*, I suggest ways in which experience-based writing might serve in academic writing by presenting a variety of illustrative published and student essays. In my discussion, I assume that accounts of personal experience will be understood as socially and culturally mediated reconstructions of context-bound events. Although self-referential discourse suggests writing of and by a coherent, fully conscious "individual," today most critics and life writers hold more sophisticated views about autobiography, experience, and evidence. As Paul John Eakin explains, a postmodern approach to life writing genres "recognizes that autobiography is necessarily in its deepest sense a special kind of fiction, its self and its truth as much created as (re)discovered realities" (*Touching* 25).

Furthermore, I acknowledge my role as "reader" in "constructing" the texts I will be analyzing and stress that my construal of these texts is not meant to suggest a single interpretation or an inherent location of meaning. However, as I hope that other academic writers and composition teachers are persuaded to adopt certain forms of personal writing, I will sometimes attribute to the writer strategic interventions that I realize have more to do with my reading than with any actual authorial intention.

Because *Personally Speaking* addresses the value of personal writing for both scholars and students, it will be of interest to composition theorists and writing instructors in both four-year and two-year institutions as well as to secondary-school English teachers who would like to move narrative from its current site as confessional writing to the domain of academic discourse. The conflict over personal writing in composition studies is most clearly manifest in classrooms, where writing teachers must decide whether to emphasize expressivist or social constructionist approaches to their instruction. By examining the constructed nature of personal accounts and lived experience, by foregrounding the semifiction in personal narratives and the rhetoricity of evidence, I hope to further complicate and intensify this pedagogical debate by suggesting even greater generic blending and blurring.

Throughout this book, I take a fairly eclectic approach, drawing not only from scholarship in composition and rhetoric but also, significantly, from feminist theory and classical rhetoric. While, at first glance, the invocation of feminism and Aristotle within the same argument might seem paradoxical, I take my authority (as I did in my earlier research on the personal) from Joy Ritchie and Kate Ronald's assertion that traditional rhetoric might be usefully "recovered" for contemporary analysis. In every chapter, I provide samples from student and published writing that reflect particular features of personal writing. When I began this project, models of personal academic argument, aside from ethnographic scholarship, were quite rare (although they are starting to appear more frequently). And so, in many cases, I have referred to personal narratives and more traditional personal essays.

Chapter 1, "What Is Personal Academic Writing?," begins by defining the somewhat ambiguous and often controversial terms *personal writing, academic discourse,* and *argument* as I intend to use them in my project. Significantly, I press for a more broad-based and antiagonistic definition of *argument,* one that allows for greater receptivity to personal accounts. As I review the central debates over experience-based writing—arguments for and against personal experience in student writing and in our own work as scholars using academic discourse—I try to be fair to both sides, to highlight the advantages celebrated by proponents and to reflect the justified concerns of the more skeptical. I also examine the movements and ideas that have led to increased acceptance of experiential evidence, although I acknowledge that the issues are far from settled, and I offer a scholarly model of personal academic argument. I conclude this chapter by considering the limits of the personal in terms of its propriety for academic discourse.

The debates over personal writing have influenced my organizational approach, for these differences result from the conflictual philosophies and viewpoints that underpin the key terms in my title. Hence, in chapters 2, 3, and 4, I artificially separate *personal, experience,* and *evidence* in order to interrogate the philosophical and pedagogical implications of each concept.

In chapter 2, "The Personal Is Rhetorical," I argue for the notion of "the personal" as a rhetorical construct. I show that while personal writing has been challenged because of its confessional implications and embraced (in some arenas) for its political implications, it is, first and foremost, a "made" thing, used to serve specific purposes. If we appreciate postmodern theories of subject formation, we recognize that even in their personal accounts, writers do not have recourse to an "authentic," independent, or centered self and, thus, that the *I* of a narrative is already a writerly construct. In this way, we can settle once and for all the "problem" of autonomous subjectivity in personal writing and appreciate instead its rhetorical agency.

In chapter 3, "Constructing Experience," I stress the constructed and interpretive nature of experiential discourse. I show that the experiential account is the rehearsal of an event that has been perceived through and rendered in language in particular, determined ways. Further, using published and student texts, I illustrate the ways that any articulation of experience will be modified, reconstituted, and fictionalized; it will be a recreation, a "story."

In chapter 4, "Valuing Personal Evidence," I suggest that by blending personal and academic discourses, meaning is extended and developed, and I address in detail the emergence of *surplus* meaning as one significant outcome of composing personal academic arguments. Further, Kenneth Burke's and Walter Fisher's orientation theories contribute to my notion of surplus and help me to demonstrate how superimposing an academic orientation on a personal narrative can produce a new and more complicated appreciation of both perspectives. Classical and narrative theorists provide useful ways to evaluate the logic and validity of personal accounts. I discuss these theories in some detail and apply them to two sample essays about responding to student writing.

As its title suggests, chapter 5, "Teaching Personal Academic Argument," offers strategies for teaching college students to evoke personal experience in their academic essays and articles. Using my own first-year writing classes as a starting point, I trace two instructional approaches: first I explain how to move students from personal to academic discourse; then I explain how to move students from academic to personal discourse. For both methods, I provide a number of student essays as samples. I also suggest strategies for foregrounding the necessary fictivity of narrative subjectivity and experience and conclude with comments about the future of personal academic argument, especially in more public arenas.

We really can live with contradictions, as postmodernists suggest, and by holding, simultaneously, opposite (or at least different) perspectives—for example, personal and academic, narrative and "rational," expressivist and social constructionist—we may arrive at richer and more complex understandings of the issues we choose to investigate. I hope that *Personally Speaking* will contribute to acceptance of the personal as evidence in academic discourse and to greater blurring of genres in academic writing.

Acknowledgments

As every teacher of undergraduate composition knows, few books in this field are written without the support of the institutions and individuals who give us time to write. I am grateful to Carl Lovitt, Ken Fifer, and Susan Speece at Penn State Berks–Lehigh Valley College and the office of the provost at Penn State University for allowing me time to invent and complete *Personally Speaking,* first through research and development grants and later through sabbatical leave.

My thanks also go to the editor of the Studies in Writing and Rhetoric series, Robert Brooke, for his encouragement and good will as I struggled to find the right voice for this project, and to Bruce Ballenger and Smokey Wilson for their careful reading and most helpful suggestions. I also thank the review committee for the Studies in Writing and Rhetoric series and the editorial team at Southern Illinois University Press, with special thanks to Karl Kageff for his assistance in the publishing process and to Wayne Larsen for his careful copyediting of my manuscript. I am indebted to Jeanne Gunner for publishing my article "Argument and Evidence in the Case of the Personal" in *College English* and the college committee of NCTE for honoring that article with the Richard Ohmann Award. The support of these people gave me confidence to further pursue the project of personal academic writing.

I thank *College English* and *JAC* for allowing me to use material from the following previously published articles of mine: "Argument and Evidence in the Case of the Personal," *College English* 64 (2001): 63–87 (copyright 2001 by the National Council of Teachers of English; reprinted with permission); and "Teaching Expressive Writing as a Narrative Fiction," *JAC: A Journal of Composition Research* 16.1 (Winter 1996): 119–40.

I am enormously grateful to my student Michelle Grider for her willingness to share her thoughts, her time, and her effort in revising her drafts; for teaching me so much about teaching writing; and for giving me permission to reprint her essay, "Nature's Lessons," as an appendix. Likewise, I thank my many students who allowed me to study their essays. Thanks too to Betsy Spigelman for transcribing tapes and proofreading chapters. I owe a debt of gratitude to my colleague Laurie Grobman, who read endless drafts of this entire manuscript, debated my arguments, and kept me on track. In this academic life, I have been most fortunate to find such a good friend. Finally, I acknowledge Michael Spigelman for giving me every kind of time I needed to write this book.

Personally Speaking

1 / What Is Personal Academic Writing?

Michelle and I sit side by side at my office desk, working on her essay "Nature's Lessons." As my first-year writing class assignment requires, Michelle has chosen two nature essays with intersecting themes and is attempting to "discuss the similarities between the texts or the ways in which the essays come together to support the same central point." In this first draft, a comparison of Louise Erdrich's "Skunk Dreams" and Annie Dillard's "Living Like Weasels," she has explained each writer's desire to live like the animal she describes. Michelle's essay is short and undeveloped but reveals a number of key insights. She writes, for example,

> Both authors are telling us that there is so much out there that people never realize or never get to experience because they are too busy dealing with the things that keep them in their "cages." . . . Erdrich is saying that she doesn't even realize the fence or barrier is there anymore[, j]ust as many people in the world today forget that they have other options.

We stop reading there.

I am impressed with the depth of Michelle's understanding and with her ability to articulate complex concepts. But as I try to probe further, to encourage additional analysis and more direct engagement with the readings, Michelle begins to repeat what she's already said. She recounts the similarities between skunk and weasel, similarities between Erdrich's and Dillard's yearnings. "But what is your point?" I ask again, "Why are you telling me about these writers, these animals, these 'cages'?" Michelle is too smart to answer

"Because it was assigned," but she is frustrated and a little confused. I need to figure out a way to help her locate her meaning without imposing my own reading. Glancing farther down the page, I find the solution. Michelle has written,

> A lot of people that we associate with create a nature of their own, to sort of make up for the nature that they don't get to experience in the outdoors. In my home, we have skylights that light up the house in the summer time and bring the sunlight to us when we just don't feel like being outside. My mother loves to have plants in the house; she takes care of them everyday and makes sure that she doesn't kill them. We have even raised a mini garden in our backyard. I guess it makes us feel close to nature and we say that we are "nature people" by having these things and enjoying the outdoors, but I think, like a lot of people, we are just fooling ourselves.

Michelle's essay is supposed to analyze two published texts to make an academic argument, yet here, smack in the middle, is this wonderful discussion of how it works in Michelle's own life. The writing seems animated, alive. More important, it does the same intellectual work as Erdrich's and Dillard's essays do: it uses first-person details to reflect (on) general human behavior. So I am faced with a dilemma. Do I tell Michelle to remove this paragraph, or do I instruct her to write a personal essay? Why, I wonder, must I—or Michelle—make a choice?

Here then is my rationale for *Personally Speaking*: without losing sight of postmodern epistemological questions, that is, without naïveté or uncritical consciousness, we in composition studies must be cautious about choosing sides—personal versus academic writing, expressivist versus social constructivist teaching—for all around us, experiential writing is already serving the needs of critical cultural examination. Personal writing can do serious academic work; it can make rational arguments; it can merge appropriately with academic discourse. Indeed, this "blended genre" is starting to appear in our professional literature, although it has not made its way into many college classrooms. Nevertheless, the problem of the personal remains controversial, in large part, I think, because those on either side of the debate aren't answering each other's questions but are instead passionately speaking past each other.

In *Personally Speaking,* I want to take another tack—to see what we gain by combining the very different "orientations" or worldviews imposed by personal and academic discourse as *personal academic discourse.* This blended approach creates useful contradictions, contributes more complicated meanings, and so may provoke greater insights than reading or writing either experiential or academic modes separately. I label this effect *surplus* and describe it as the "excessive" consequence of simultaneously viewing an issue from alternate perspectives.

I recognize that appeals to personal experience *as* evidence lead, inevitably, to complex, paradoxical questions, which I will try to address from the inside out. Sometimes I will interrogate theories, sometimes I will analyze texts, sometimes I will locate my concerns in my first year writing classroom. Always my purpose is twofold: to legitimize personal writing for its opponents and to expose to supporters the scholarly and political complexities of experiential discourse. In the end, I hope that compositionists will appreciate more fully personal academic writing and in doing so become both more receptive to and more critically conscious of what this genre has to offer us and our students. Ultimately, I want to help Michelle find a way to make *her* argument.

The Scope of Personal Writing

In the following pages, I talk a great deal about *personal writing,* so I need to explain from the start that I am using this term, as well as *experiential writing* and *personal narrative,* to refer to the ways in which writers make sense of their lives by organizing their experience into first-person stories. As interest in personal writing grows, so do the many labels used to describe it: *life writing, self-writing, autobiographical account, memoir, personal reference,* some types of *creative nonfiction,* and even, in Karen Surman Paley's phrase, *I-writing.* These terms mark the kind of discourse that calls into play a writer's lived experiences as well as his or her reflections about these experiences. But definitions often fail to encompass the nuances of these genres; categories overlap and run together, often replicating form while differing in purpose.

The scope of personal writing is indeed far-reaching. Probably most familiar (to those of us who love creative nonfiction, as well as to students who are assigned such readings) is the tightly focused, carefully plotted narrative characteristic of many contemporary personal essays. Alice Walker's "Beauty: When the Other Dancer Is the Self" illustrates this type of experience-based prose. Walker chronicles events that led to a childhood accident with a pellet gun, a pivotal moment of disfigurement to both the narrator's eye and her self-esteem; then the "story" continues, relating the series of incidents in her personal life that culminated in self-acceptance and emotional healing. In contrast are personal narratives in which the narrator's experience is woven into a tapestry of reflections about more public concerns. Typical of this approach are "Aria," a literacy narrative in *Hunger of Memory* that depicts young Richard Rodriguez's struggle to accommodate his Spanish language of home, family, and comfort with the austere expression of American English, and E. B. White's "Sootfall and Fallout," in which the personal is used as a frame to speculate on pollution and nuclear power.[1]

Although extended personal narratives generally do not appear in academic articles, scholarly writers are starting to appropriate the rich possibilities of detail and multiple perspectives characteristic of such writing, and increasingly, academics are using personal writing for cultural critical purposes. Such efforts are most fully realized in the kind of writing that is sometimes called "autoethnography," autobiographical accounts like Victor Villanueva's *Bootstraps,* Linda Brodkey's "Writing on the Bias," and Mike Rose's *Lives on the Boundary.* By embedding their personal stories into contexts in which race, class, gender, and other constructs are made visible, these writers seek to subvert traditional political and cultural associations relating to autonomous subjectivity. Autoethnographic writing insists that the narrative of an individual's life is both the product and process of surrounding social and educational narratives. Patricia J. Williams's *The Alchemy of Race and Rights* takes personal narrative even further, combining academic and autobiographical writing to argue legal theory.

For many composition teachers, the distinctions among *personal essay, personal narrative,* and *personal experience writing* are particularly slippery, owing in some measure to the differences between what students have been taught to produce and what essayists and scholars of the essay mean when they talk about that genre. For example, the term *personal narrative* may designate the practice of *free writing,* in other words, writing for the self, writing used to find or construct meaning with or without autobiographical reference. Sometimes, too, it is used to describe developing writers' chronologies of confession or insight. Contrasting the form of writing associated most closely with writers like Michel de Montaigne, Charles Lamb, E. B. White, and Joan Didion with classroom products, Dana C. Elder observes that students who are asked to write personal essays in their English classes

> believe that what the teacher wants is a narrative in which each student reveals some secret shame or misfortune—in vivid detail . . . [or they] believe that what is required is an autobiographical incident with a "moral" tagged onto the end of it. (425–26)[2]

These are *not* the types of personal writing I have in mind. Because I want to focus on the rhetoric of the personal, I turn instead to Paley's explanation of personal narrative, which comes closer to my sense of the genre.

> Personal narrative takes the writer's own experience as its focus. It involves the use of a narrational *I* that seems to be the actual voice of the person who writes. Sometimes the narrator may appear to isolate individual consciousness, and sometimes he or she may represent the self in one

or more social contexts, such as the family or college community. The narrator may or may not explicitly link the
particular situation with those experienced by others. (13)

Paley's definition stresses that writing is representation; she reminds
us that rhetorical appearance differs from reality. Her last sentence
also implies that the reader has a distinct role in completing the
inferential leap from the particularities of the textual reference to
his or her own lived experiences.

The varied and intersecting definitions of the personal make it
possible for me to use *personal writing, experiential writing,* and
personal narrative somewhat interchangeably throughout this book.
However, I want to emphasize that although writers may organize
their stories of experience into single sentences or as lengthy chro-
nological accounts, in the kind of personal writing I have in mind,
the telling is *purposeful* and intended to do more than express an
opinion or cathartically confess. As I hope to show, my view of personal writing takes into account both expressivist and social constructionist concerns and makes it possible for me to teach Michelle,
in the words of Alan France, "to translate public knowledge into
personal meaning—and back again" (164).

The Scope of Academic Writing

It often seems as if we speak of *academic writing* as the default concept, the standard discourse and the standard practice for first-year
composition classes. But *academic discourse* is itself a contested and
confusing term. Does it describe the citation-laden articles of university faculty, representing genre conventions of particular disciplines? If so, as many have suggested, we need to talk about academic *discourses,* since each discipline has its own conventions and
requirements. In most scholarly articles in composition studies (the
field I can speak of with greatest authority), textual source and reference are at once the bases from which to develop new and more
complicated insights and the way in which writers establish their
authority, by conveying their appreciation and understanding of

prior research.³ Yet we would all agree that academic discourse involves more than attribution; it reflects (or at least we expect it to reflect) deep engagement with these prior accounts or, as we say, conversations among members of academic discourse communities. In the 1980s, compositionists debated at length what student writers needed to know to be successful in their college classes. In contrast to the set formulas of current-traditional instruction and the free-ranging, voice-centered theories of expressivist instruction, some theorists proposed explicit instruction in academic discourse, a pedagogy that was intended to "demystify the conventions of the academic discourse community" (Bizzell, "Cognition" 370). Writing instructors soon came to recognize, however, the social, political, and ethical implications of this approach. They noted that students, like almost everyone, speak and write myriad discourses from a number of complementary and contradictory locations, both literal and figurative, that "the borders of most discourses are hazily marked and often traveled, and that the communities they define are thus often indistinct and overlapping" (J. Harris, *Teaching* 103). In "The Idea of Community in the Study of Writing," Joseph Harris cautioned that the very notion of academic discourse community risked constituting speakers and writers as inside or outside privileged discourse groups. Such practice, he has reminded us, not only tends to solidify particular, arbitrary aspects of a discourse but, more significantly, raises questions about how and why students might want to learn this discourse in the first place (*Teaching* 97–107). Keeping these concerns in mind, I define *academic writing* and other associated terms quite broadly, but I do so with awareness of their history and their varied significations.

A great many composition teachers would characterize academic discourse as rhetorical *argument*, a thesis-driven essay written in third-person point of view using a deductive (or possibly inductive) structure of claim and support (with or without source texts). For others, traditional and advanced research techniques and meaningful integration of sources are requisite for arguments appropriate to college writing. Still, many teachers view as academic writing any nonnarrative text that attempts to examine, analyze, or interrogate a topic.

The writing itself is not necessarily formal, but the tone is somewhat serious. In this sense, the traditional essay (as opposed to the personal narrative) could be considered academic discourse.

In *Personally Speaking,* I include all of these notions of academic writing and use the terms *academic discourse, academic argument,* and *scholarly writing* to reflect these broad and overlapping categories. My model of academic writing instruction involves students' engagement with texts beyond their own, but my view of this discourse is centrally generic. I discuss the debate between expressivist and academic discourse proponents below. In chapter 5, as I suggest ways to teach students to fruitfully invoke their personal experiences as evidence, I present student essays that illustrate various kinds of academic writing. Like all terms, *academic discourse* is polysemous, politically charged, and always problematic. If my arguments are successful, readers will view academic writing as both more intricate and more flexible.

Argument in Academic Writing

For many composition scholars today, the notion of argument is contentious. Rhetorical argument is assumed to be competitive, combative, hierarchical, oppressive, and thus antithetical to personal and narrative genres. I want to look critically at this conception of argument as I propose a more embracing, epistemic conception of our goals in academic writing. In my view, personal narrative, in its various forms, should be understood as a logical and legitimate mode of argument. At the same time, I look forward to modifications in the legacy of traditional argument as a result of using experience-based evidence in academic discourse.

In composition literature, the argument-narrative dichotomy is often grounded in gender, the rhetorically masculine thesis-driven essay contrasted with the rhetorically feminine personal essay. For example, Paul Heilker asserts that

[w]hile the thesis/support form encourages the use of a primarily masculine thinking and discourse, emphasizing

an abstract, logical, impersonal, rational, linear, agonistic,
framed, contained, preselected, and packaged thinking and
discourse that presses for explicitness and closure, the essay celebrates an opposing feminine rhetoric (sensual, con-
textual, committed, intuitive, associative, holistic, indirect,
open-ended, generative, less processed, and less controlled)
that values implicitness, multiplicity, simultaneity, open-
ness, and inclusion. (165)

Although feminist scholarship has done much to describe and
value various patterns of thinking and writing, revealing that men
and women are acculturated to use and prefer different styles of
discourse,[4] there seems to me certain danger in the kind of essen-
tializing (and demonizing) that makes women's rhetoric inherently
soft and men's inherently rigorous. Indeed, even as she suggests an
alternative approach to the combative methods long associated with
"masculine" discourse, Olivia Frey urges that we "set aside, probably indefinitely, the question of what is natural for women to do,
that is, the question of woman's essential nature." To avoid "false
generalizations" about gender, she recommends that we "contextualize our discussions" of particular women (and men) by describing their specific political, social, and cultural positions (519).[5]
While acknowledging that argument is not "essentially" masculine,
feminists and literary critics have sought alternatives to the agonistic
rhetoric traditionally associated with academic argument and male-
dominant discourse. They have posited, instead, exploratory models that embrace, rather than contest, opposing positions.[6]

In general, however, academic arguments seem far less aggres-
sively motivated. In fact, most scholarship bears a striking contrast
to the traditional characterization of argument with its associated
model of domination. According to Richard Fulkerson, typical academic writers use some of the conventions of argument, such as
citing authorities, offering critiques of opposing views, and providing evidence and examples, not to impose their position but rather
to offer their readers an idea in the hope that they may "find it believable and worth adopting" (204–5). In the view of many theo-

rists, the claims and supports we use to make academic arguments appear in all kinds of writing and speaking formations, from history reports to poetic interpretations to ethnographic research. Andrea A. Lunsford and John J. Ruszkiewicz observe that "from the morning news to the AIDS ribbon, from the American flag to the Nike swoosh, we are surrounded by texts that beckon, that aim to persuade. . . . [Hence,] *everything* is an argument" (iii, emphasis in original). Using poems, informative essays, visual media, and so on, their composition text demonstrates that arguments are not necessarily about winning and losing but are sometimes designed to "invite others to enter a space of mutual regard and exploration" (5).[7]

In most academic settings, the give-and-take in scholarly discourse communities promotes the exchange and advancement of disciplinary knowledge. Claims and counterarguments are epistemically motivated: they constitute dialectical interactions aimed at "reaching some mutually enlightening understanding" (Fulkerson 212; 211–13). I find this explanation satisfying because it is consistent with my experience of English studies scholarship. Except for occasional comment-and-response articles, most of what I read in composition journals and books does indeed posit positions, provide evidence, and investigate alternative stances, but the effort seems more collegial than combative, more focused on enlarging rather than contesting others' claims or points of view.[8] As our particular method of argument reinforces the expansiveness of academic discourse and suggests the possibility of including personal writing within its domain, for my purposes it seems appropriate to retain both the term and the idea of *academic argument*.

Making Way for Personal Academic Argument

Historically, both ethnographic and feminist models of research have influenced personal writing in composition scholarship. Ethnographic methods in anthropology, linguistics, sociology, and education honor experience and recognize the importance of recording and examining the events that shape the lives of social participants.

Since the late 1980s, with the shift from cognitive psychology's protocol analysis to methodologies associated with the social construction of knowledge and sociolinguistics, composition research has drawn on ethnographic methods (Brodkey, "Writing Ethnographic" 36–38). Bearing on current attitudes toward ethnography is the recognition that "experience is not—indeed, cannot be—reproduced in speech or writing, and must instead be narrated" (26). The ethnographer's intrusiveness in the study setting and his or her biases and interpretive stance are all foregrounded (30–32).[9] Ethnographies are often written in first person, and case studies exploit narrative techniques not only for their aesthetic effects but also to underscore the social constructedness of the research itself (Bishop, "Students'" 202–03). Contemporary ethnographic methods not only have influenced the way compositionists report their research but also have encouraged greater use of personal reference in all types of scholarly writing.

Feminist scholarship has also influenced composition research and writing practices, especially in the last decade. Calling attention to the writer's choice of using the collective "we" versus the "I" of personal narrative, Lynn Worsham notes that "since the personal is first and always political (and therefore transubjective), personal pronouns may sometime serve a collective function" ("After Words" 336). With this purpose in mind, compositionists have used personal experience to counter gender discrimination, to encourage consciousness-raising, and to oppose and resist oppressive pedagogies, department politics, and research practices (Ritchie and Boardman). Joy Ritchie and Kathleen Boardman include Adrienne Rich's "When We Dead Awaken: Writing as Re-Vision," Joan Bolker's "Teaching Griselda to Write," Lynn Z. Bloom's "Teaching College English as a Woman," and Min-Zhan Lu's "Conflict and Struggle: The Enemies or Preconditions of Basic Writing?" among the narrative essays that have had a significant impact on composition theory and practice. We should also include Mary Field Belenky, Blythe McVicker Clinchy, Nancy Rule Goldberger, and Jill Mattuck Tarule's *Women's Ways of Knowing,* which, with its examples drawn from the transcripts of actual research subjects, has been a model for the use of personal narratives in case research.

Frey's 1990 *College English* article shows feminists in composition calling into question the discipline's use of academic argument as "adversarial," opting for more personal and open-ended forms of scholarly discourse. Moreover, in 1992, Lynn Z. Bloom challenged notions of how academic essays could be written in "Teaching College English as a Woman," as did Nancy Sommers in "Between the Drafts." Projects such as these paved the way for publications like Sheryl I. Fontaine and Susan Hunter's *Writing Ourselves into the Story*, a collection of essays about teaching writing dedicated to the personal perspectives, or "unheard voices," of writing instructors who view themselves as outside mainstream theory building.

In recent years, composition scholars in some arenas have taken a dramatic turn toward the personal and experiential, with events like the 1999 NCTE Conference, "Stories in the Classroom: Narration as Knowledge," in Tucson. As the keynote speaker, Joseph Trimmer received strong support when he criticized the professional enculturation that has made so many composition scholars distrust stories (both literary and anecdotal) in favor of theory and interpretation. Like Fontaine and Hunter's edition, the essays in Trimmer's *Narration as Knowledge: Tales of the Teaching Life* construct a collective argument for the value and importance of personal experience. These collections represent early inroads in favor of the personal in academic publications. However, changes are continuing, most evidenced in recent publications like Paley's *I-Writing: The Politics and Practice of Teaching First-Person Writing*, an ethnographic analysis of and argument for expressive writing instruction, and Barbara Kamler's *Relocating the Personal: A Critical Writing Pedagogy*, a collection of strategies for teaching personal writing as narrative in various academic settings. Important collections also include Deborah H. Holdstein and David Bleich's *Personal Effects: The Social Character of Scholarly Writing* and two dedicated volumes from *College English*, both guest edited by Jane E. Hindman, "Personal Writing" in September 2001 and "The Personal in Academic Writing" in September 2003.

Limits to Personal Access

In general, however, opportunities for personal writing in academic discourse still tend to be confined to those who have already paid their professional dues (an exception being the increase in personal narratives in recent volumes of *Teaching English in the Two-Year College [TETYC]*, under Howard Tinberg's editorship). Discussing ethnographic projects and the freedom of the "I-witnessing" voice, Wendy Bishop addresses directly the scholar's earned "right" to speak. Bishop points out that if, in ethnographic research, validity depends on the constructed author, then only those who have established themselves within the discipline may experiment with ethical and emotional appeals, by virtue of their having already developed a recognized and accepted ethos within the community. In 1987, Bishop recognized that such avenues were not open to graduate students writing dissertations. Again in 1998, Joy Ritchie's student Thelma observed in her journal that only those academics who had achieved "a certain status of establishment, respectability, and safety" could experiment with alternative forms of written discourse (Ritchie and Ronald 236). Deborah Holdstein likewise invokes the notion of entitlement, observing that it is still the case that only those who have "mastered . . . the various rhetorics of academe . . . [have] *earned the right to be personal*" (7–8, emphasis in original). Holdstein expresses the view of many in our field: "more often than not . . . being 'too' personal is a luxury, the privilege of those who have somehow arrived" (9).[10]

Frequently, too, those who most value personal writing cast it in opposition to either academic discourse or social constructionist models (which are not necessarily one and the same). In *I-Writing*, for example, Paley insists that both James Berlin and Lester Faigley inaccurately characterize expressivist writing pedagogy as an approach that posits individual, private vision, precludes tolerance for alternative viewpoints, and naively ignores postmodern conceptions of subject formation. To redeem expressivism, she engages in a critique of her own, defending expressivism against its social-constructionist objectors while undermining their critical assertions as she constructs them.[11]

It's true that the question of the personal in composition remains stunningly political. Scholars who prize the telling of personal stories for their colleagues may emphatically oppose writing instruction that would allow the same for students (Bloom, "Why Don't"; Bishop, "Suddenly" 271). From the opposite side, they may allow for personal writing instruction for students but claim, as Joseph Harris does, that it is inappropriate to academic discourse, which demands more direct and focused attention to the scholarly topic ("Person" 51–2). But promoting one genre at the expense of the other does not solve the problem. As Debbie Mutnick observes, in classroom contexts a polarized perspective ultimately "does students a disservice by truncating writing instruction . . . . [and] imposing artificial limits on attempts to make sense out of complex experience" (80).

It seems to me that there is greater advantage to blending discourses: using personal writing in and as academic argument. In support of this view, many writing theorists, including those who initially supported a strong academic discourse orientation, now cast their vote in favor of more "hybrid" or experimental forms, which may better prepare students for writing in multiple contexts (for example, Bizzell, "Hybrid" 8). In Patricia Bizzell's view, exploiting varied generic conventions—including informal language, subjectivity, emotional expression, consensus building, cultural and personal references—encourages new ways of thinking and richer modes of scholarship ("Hybrid" 11–17). This blended form, which I am calling *personal academic argument,* is beginning to emerge, albeit in limited venues, in the social sciences, literary criticism, and composition studies. Why and how these arguments succeed rhetorically are central concerns in the chapters that follow.

Personal Academic Argument: A Model for Composition

What does an argument drawn from personal experience look like? Can we actually create texts that fully integrate the genres of personal narrative and academic argument? At this juncture, we have only a few models for this type of scholarship, which rhetorically challenges and tests the limits of scientific demands for logical proof. However, Lynn Worsham's "After Words: A Choice of Words Remains" provides a splendid example. Unlike most other academic essays that incorporate narrative, Worsham's academic discourse frames the personal and the fictive, instead of the other way around. Indeed, the stories themselves are so crucial to the essay's internal structure that they cannot be bracketed without dismantling the argument itself.

In her essay, Worsham calls for current generations of feminists to put aside divisive attitudes intended to "expose the blindness of one feminism and the fraudulence of another" (351). To fight oppression and effect social change, Worsham says, feminists must "forge a collective subject capable of making mass movement— . . . an alliance that does not protect us from our differences but finds in difference, disagreement, and even despair occasions to hear one another's words" (329). The choice of the infinitive *to hear* is not incidental, for Worsham builds her argument for action by telling a series of stories, allowing us to model, as we read, the intellectually active, generous listening required for just such collective subject formation.

Worsham draws from the fictional and the experiential to make her case. She begins by reflecting on Toni Morrison's 1993 Nobel Prize speech, a lesson in life choices and the power of language to shape and reshape action, presented as an extended metaphor. As she retells Morrison's fictional narrative of the blind seer and the young people who challenge her with their hidden bird, asking "Is the bird . . . living or dead?" (qtd. in Worsham, "After Words" 331), Worsham reminds readers that Morrison's bird is language and that it holds all generations equally responsible for the "word work" that is powerful enough "both to secure difference and to make a shareable world" (332).

Her second narrative is personal, a family memoir: the account of "Blue Betty" provides a story of her own life, both made and fixed in language. According to Worsham, in an effort to question the arbitrariness of racial and gender constructions, her mother repeatedly told how, as a child, Lynn confused the words *colored* and *blue* to describe her African American caretaker. As a young adult,

Worsham explains, she came to hate the story, recognizing its exploitative and ethnocentric dimensions, although it continued to haunt her.

Worsham's third story is visual as well as narrative, constructed as it is from a photograph of her maternal grandmother, a Native American, whose race and class remained a well-kept family secret. By piecing together her mother's past, itself a tale of racial and class identity construction, she is able to find a way back through the "door" of the tale of Blue Betty, to appreciate it simultaneously from her mother's historical reality, from Betty's, and from her own, and to see the relationship, the interconnectedness, between these configurations. In this final story, she emphasizes that all of our perspectives, viewpoints, and memories are already drenched in "emotional coloration, that they are patterns of feeling—orchestrated in historically specific ways by categories of gender, race, class, and sexuality—that give an affective shape to experience and the stories we tell" (340).

Worsham's stories serve as examples, specific cases of generational conflict from which her audience can generalize about the state of contemporary feminism. She clearly assumes that her readers, largely feminists in composition studies, represent various alliances in academic feminism, that they are all committed to advancing women's liberation, and that they share a common understanding of feminist scholarship. The collective dream of the "third wave," suggesting a galvanized political response, unites the audience and promotes the kind of community necessary for deliberative action. Each story has its own individual logic, or rational appeal; each in its own way argues for generational understanding, tolerance, and responsibility.

At the same time, Worsham establishes ethos by citing other respected writers and researchers. Demonstrating her own generous appreciation of the literature and its application to the current situation, her text and her reputation in the field mark her as an established scholar worthy of our respect and trust. Emotion and sympathy are aroused by means of the text's own "word work," not only a tenderness expressed toward the "characters" in each of her stories but a sensitive embrace of the audience who participates in weaving the tapestry together in order to understand its implications.

Personal Evidence and Academic Appropriateness

"After Words" is satisfying on a number of levels, not the least of which is its appropriateness as academic writing. For decades, scholars and teachers have debated the efficacy of self-disclosure in "public" discourse for a number of ethical, philosophical, and practical reasons. Indeed, the need for this book is testimony to the irreconcilability of claims on both sides of the issue. Yet opponents and proponents are united in their apprehension that disclosure of personal experience risks self-indulgence or exploitation. How do we grade a poorly executed essay about a brother killed by a drunk driver? How do we tell a rape victim that her scenic paragraph needs revising? Inviting confessional, emotional, or experiential writing into the classroom to be shared and evaluated requires not only great sensitivity but also recognition of one's own powerful position. Moreover, in our own writing, a revealing self-disclosure can fortify an academic argument, or it can distract from or confuse the terms of the debate.

An appreciation of appropriateness offers a partial remedy for such concerns about personal disclosure. We can benefit from studying essays and research articles that "use personal background, experiences, and perceptions—sometimes via narratives—in critical ways, making public what could be taken as private for professional purposes" (Herrington 48–49). For example, the genre of "critical autobiography," as Villanueva describes it, demonstrates appropriate use of the personal: elements of autobiography may serve "not as confession and errant self-indulgence, not as the measure on which to assess theory, not as a replacement for rigor, but as a way of knowing our predispositions to see things certain ways, of understanding what it is that guides our intuitions in certain ways" ("Personal" 51).

We can ask, as Suzanne Clark does, whether judging the personal inappropriate to academic discourse reflects the age-old desire to free writing from emotional contamination, a masculinist longing for an ideal discourse of pure reason and facticity, a discourse free of rhetoric. According to Clark, because the privilege of reason over emotion is so entrenched in academic discourse conventions, academics fear any form of expression that suggests sentimentality. She shows that the aversion to sentimentality developed as the emerging eighteenth-century middle class divided discourse categories: public and private, political and domestic, male and female, rational and emotional. Irrational emotion was linked to the female, to sentimentality, and ultimately to hysteria ("Rhetoric").

Today, Clark argues, we should realize that both reason and emotion are artificial distinctions. Since all knowledge is socially constructed, we have no recourse to the coherent identity of a subject that can define "the rational." As such, we must acknowledge the mutuality of logic, audience, and speaker, and the value of sentiment as an expression of shared concern within a rhetorical community ("Rhetoric"). Furthermore, according to Worsham, if we regard emotion therapeutically, viewing it as purely private and individual, we conceal the cultural work of ideology, specifically its efforts to silence collective emotional response to injustice and oppression ("Coming" 106–10).

From a different vantage point, we can also question whether the American tradition of privatizing certain kinds of lived experience, long noted by feminists, has produced paradoxical effects: the simultaneous horror and allure of personal disclosure. Decades of suppressing personal issues may account for the rebound effect most visible today in media-sponsored confessional and victimization rhetoric. In recent years, we've witnessed a crush of popular forums in which personal disclosure, testimony, and confession seem to have become central modes of entertainment. Television talks shows and "reality TV" are staples of every major commercial network. Popular memoirs (with provocative titles like *My Life as Elvis*) have become a best-selling genre. Some critics attribute the increased appeal of the personal to voyeuristic titillation. Others attribute to it a carnivalesque attraction akin to the sideshow, in which the talk show guest becomes the object of anti-identification, a complex process by which dominant cultural beliefs and values are reified by means of contrast, especially dangerous to minorities and women who are shown to transgress.[12]

To help us define appropriate uses of personal experience, we might turn to ancient rhetorical theories. Aristotle claims that poetic works succeed when an audience experiences what he calls *catharsis,* a heightened emotional and intellectual appreciation of a dramatic situation achieved by identifying in some way with the circumstances of the characters on stage. Similarly, in rhetorical situations, emotions may be aroused by hearing or reading speeches, since identification with the speaker or writer and the resulting empathetic pain, suffering, joy, pity, or fear can be generated on the stage, in the courthouse, or on the written page.[13] These appeals to empathy will not necessarily purge the audience's emotions but will make such emotions manifest in order to put the listener or reader in a receptive state (J. Walker 78).[14]

Worsham says that emotions generated through such textual power can bring us together as witnesses of injustice and incite in us "the kind of outrage that makes change" ("After Words" 340). Thus, in "After Words," when Worsham writes,

> When I was a child, I always hung around on the edges of adult talk until this story [of how Blue Betty got her name] was told, because it worked the way my mother intended it to work: it nourished the starving girl-child of a father who aggressively denied his daughters the power of naming and the right to choose a vision, (337)

her words do not invoke in us mere sympathy or despair for one particular child; rather they summon a collective consciousness of the social conditions that perpetuate impotence (and the exigency of story) in girls' and women's lives.

Aristotle also insists that effective rhetors will not stimulate passionate, nonreflective response for its own sake. In his view, we must combine emotion with reason and ethics to make judicious decisions (J. Walker 91). In personal academic argument, then, we must consider the "timeliness" and "appropriateness" of emotion-laden disclosures. Aristotle maintains that the choice and use of strategies will depend on the subject under discussion, the occasion, and the speaker's identity or deemed role at a particular occasion.[15] Worsham makes it clear that her decision to share private family stories does not come easily. Although the account of Blue Betty has long been a cause of emotional and cognitive dissonance ("something in the story . . . that feels like a question"), she recognizes in it a shameful disclosure ("'the real thing' I would change a whole history . . . in order to disavow") ("After Words" 335).

Nevertheless, relating this tale is both timely and appropriate. Addressing schisms in contemporary American feminism, she wants to illustrate how to read "generational differences and connections dialectically as they take place specifically across the stress points of gender, race, and class" ("After Words" 335). This critical moment in feminism and the particular venue of *Feminism and Composition Studies* offer the right occasion to disclose, for as Worsham explains,

> Working through this story here—wording it as my mother did and rewording it with terms offered in this volume—represents a provisional response to feminists of color who have challenged me (and, indeed, all white feminists) to tell the truth and be accountable, to name the enemy within, and to examine the specificities of the role race has played in this white life. ("After Words" 335)

Earlier in this chapter, we saw that Worsham's personal reflections contributed to the construction of her arguments. Here we note that they also contribute to the development of a context for making her case.

Worsham's essay reveals the deliberation involved in determining whether to provide a personal account or to tell an emotionally charged story. All writers must decide first whether such devices are appropriate to the argument itself or to the context in which the topic is being debated. In terms of academic publications, for example, many scholars will define as inappropriate personal renderings intended merely for self-reflection or confession (and they are equally wary of insisting on personal disclosure as a disciplinary matter of course). Initiating the September 2001 *College English* symposium debate on personal writing, Gesa Kirsch and Min-Zhan Lu caution, "Uncritical celebrations of personal narrative can risk equating a person's reluctance to shape and talk about the personal within the limits of the genre with that person's failure to recognize and/or acknowledge the personal as political" (42).

In the same article, Anne Herrington argues that we should disclose personal information in our professional writing only if it is directly relevant to the issues we are raising, but she also acknowledges the pressure that has recently been brought to bear on such accounts (47). Worsham fears a narcissistic trend in composition, an "obsession with 'the personal'" that consumes transformative emotional energy "into a form of academic writing that simply seeks self-validation" ("Coming" 112–13). Such comments underscore the relevance of appropriateness, suggesting that we must be cautious about how and why we choose to invoke personal experience.

Similarly, in our classrooms, we owe our students the right to resist disclosure (Gere) as well as assistance in deciding when personal accounts are rhetorically useful. Personal writing assignments may be judged inappropriate when student writers are asked to report personal observations, behaviors, or dialogues and then find themselves evaluated on the basis of their lives rather than their writing. In this case, the personal essay may offer a particular advantage for certain nontraditional students, whose experiences seem more colorful, or more desperate, to their middle-class teachers. On the other hand, expressive self-disclosures may be a liability if the behaviors or beliefs recounted in the student's narrative are immoral or unlawful, if they are inconsistent with the teacher's value system, or if, by the instructor's standards, the student fails to achieve "appropriate" insight regarding the significance of his or her experience (R. Miller; Faigley 408–11; Bizzell, "College" 194–95; Gere 206–07).[16]

Moreover, within particular families and cultural and ethnic groups, disclosure of the personal may be prohibited. Recall, for example, that Richard Rodriguez describes his mature autobiographical accounts as acts of "betrayal" and contrasts them with his early writing, in which, consistent with the values of his upbringing, he fictionalized school assignments that asked him to depict his family's life (177–82).

All in all, our rule of thumb should be that if an experiential account fulfills Aristotle's requirements for timeliness and suitability, then it is appropriate for the job. *Ultimately, we might say, no topic is of itself more or less appropriate to public discourse; rather it is a question of the purposes to which the topic is put and a question of the purpose that treatment of the topic serves.*

Positions and Counterpositions

Although a clearer conception of appropriateness can resolve some concerns about personal disclosure, problems with the personal remain. Indeed, the most vexing issues relating to the use of experience in academic settings hinge on crucial philosophical questions. Centrally, these questions arise from a social view of writing and from a contemporary understanding of subjective experience. In subsequent chapters, I will address at length these "problems of the personal" from a number of epistemological angles. Ultimately, I hope to show that these epistemological reservations lose much of their weight if we understand experience-based writing as rhetorical rather than referential. At this point, I'd like to begin the discussion by focusing directly on the debates about teaching personal writing in composition classrooms.

Over the decades, as composition instructors have tried out various personal writing pedagogies, they have also examined personal writing instruction in light of theories of language, of knowledge making, and of writing processes; and they have noted inconsistencies at some of these intersections. As a result of these insights, they have cautioned that asking students to invoke their lived experience in academic writing may fail to prepare them for the specialized discourses and discursive strategies they will need to be successful in, and to critique, their college classes (Bizzell, "Cognition"; S. Miller). Moreover, they have noted that metaphors that focus on students' private voices, visions, and ultimate authority over their texts can create an inaccurate and ingenuous conception of composing, where language becomes a transparent vehicle for exposing the thought processes of a unified and consistent mind at work. Such an approach, they suggest, can overemphasize the power of personal insight and ignore the ways that knowledge is constructed socially (Faigley; Bartholomae, "Writing"; Clifford).

In consequence, some theorists caution that expressive approaches to writing tend to valorize an asocial, noncollective individual (Trimbur; Berlin, *Rhetoric and Reality;* LeFevre). Asking students "to imagine that they can clear out a space to write on their own, to express their own thoughts and ideas, not to reproduce those of others," David Bartholomae argues in "Writing with Teachers: A Conversation with Peter Elbow," "is an expression of a desire for an institutional space free from institutional pressures, a cultural process free from the influence of culture, an historical moment outside of history, an academic setting free from academic writing" (64). The dream of a free space, Bartholomae contends, blinds both students and teachers to the ways that authority and power are reproduced in language and culture ("Reply" 129). Still another concern is that when we ask students (particularly white, middle-class students) to write about personal issues, we run the risk of simply reinscribing dominant cultural values that resist change and lead to stereotyping (Mutnick 84; Paley 66–83).

However, advocates know that personal writing that serves academic purposes need not be self-disclosing; neither must its ends be simply emotive and self-serving. They recall that in its 1960s to 1970s formulation, expressive writing pedagogy resulted from the good-faith efforts of many writing teachers to encourage students to find and express their individual "voices," or as Donald Stewart notes, "to escape from the pasteurized and pedestrian prose . . . [students] had been conditioned to produce in the traditional[, that is, current traditional writing] classroom" (66), particularly the hollow and formulaic five-paragraph theme. Stewart and James Berlin emphasize that expressivist rhetoric as it was taught in the sixties and seventies was "unsparingly critical of the dominant social, political, and cultural practices of the time" (Berlin, "Rhetoric and Ideology" 485). The goal of this kind of teaching was to empower students to speak their minds and to find their voices in order to express their opinions and to dissent.

Today, those who support classroom instruction in personal writing point to the ease and accessibility of expressivist discourses. They explain that narrative as form is more adaptable and readable than what they deem to be the obfuscatory theoretical writing required of most college students. Moreover, because academic writing is noticeably formal in tone and style, they see in personal writing a method for helping students to understand and clarify their academic material. At the same time, they say, personal writing encourages students to want to write for their own pleasure (Elbow, "Reflections" 136–37). Experience-based writing is thus a method for helping students to enter the academic conversation, by bringing their own extratextual knowledge and the authority of their own voices to the texts they read (Spellmeyer; Bishop, "Students'").

Also, some compositionists now assert that personal writing, when adequately theorized, is consistent with critical and political efforts to "vocalize" previously silenced voices. According to Mutnick, the life writing of traditionally marginalized groups offers members opportunities to counteract and interrogate the readings and images produced and written for them by the dominant culture. These opportunities, Mutnick insists, must be available to college students regardless of their backgrounds or affiliations. Calling for the "theorization of experience" (85), she insists that projects can be constructed to invite students to interrogate their socially and historically situated roles and identities (Mahala and Swilky) and notes that Paulo Freire argued for the subject's need to tell his or her own story to come to full consciousness.[17]

Beyond the classroom, in our own professional writing, parallel debates ensue. Although most of us enjoy reading personal accounts, in academic settings experience as evidence is generally viewed with skepticism. In the past, personal writing was considered inherently subjective and "unscientific," and thus inherently unsuitable for scholarship. Today, postmodernists question its rep-

resentation of subjects as individuals. Although contemporary critical approaches acknowledge the complex social features of any reading and thus recognize the impossibility of "impersonal" interpretation, most critical writing sustains a stance of objectivity, in part,
because postmodern theory calls into question the coherent, autonomous, humanist subject who could lay claim to his or her "personal"
experience.[18] Moreover, critiques of the myth of personal achievement that has historically undergirded American capitalism (deny-
ing social context and the associated fortunes of race, class, gender)
expose the danger of what appears to be the individual voice speaking individual experience.

Yet personal experience is not the only evidence that is subjective. We now recognize the limits of objectivity in all forms of research,
including work in literary studies and history, social science, and even
the natural sciences (e.g., Dubrow; Bazerman; Gilbert and Mulkay;
Latour and Woolgar). We know that regardless of its form in first-
person narrative or third-person exposition, all writing is personal
in the sense that both style and interest are features of social, political, and individual values and investments. Moreover, knowledge
of a researcher's social, political, and personal circumstances can
provide important information concerning his or her findings.[19]

Furthermore, many scholars find strategic advantages in personal writing. It may function as a mask in a calculated performance,
creating a reader-friendly voice and persona (Molloy 1073; Davidson
1071). Or it may operate in the service of argument as a kind of
ethos-building strategy, whereby the narrator establishes his or her
credibility by means of a voice or persona with which the audience
might identify (in Kenneth Burke's sense of the term) or trust (in
Aristotle's sense) and thus be persuaded (Boone 1152). Many writers and readers believe that personal stories are more accessible or
readable than theory (Elbow, "Reflections"). Joseph A. Boone asserts
that writing "theoretically" in a personal voice diminishes the bur-
dens imposed by writing "theory." The personal voice

> provides a provisional counter to this posturing, creating
> a relatively safe space in which to own the limits of one's

understanding, as well as to engage a level of theoretical speculation to which the language of high theory is not the sole means of access. (1153)

Finally, reviewing various disciplinary positions, Jane E. Hindman explains that supporters of the personal observe the tendency of abstract discourses to objectify both writers and subjects, stripping discourse of its "materiality." While abstract discourse "perpetuates the disciplinary will to truth," more familiar forms of writing recoup this materiality and thus acknowledge "what is at stake in the writing" (35). Most feminists and multiculturalists, as well as some other critical theorists, have come to value personal writing that gives voice to the experiences and perspectives of those who are often silenced.

This brief summary of disciplinary debates reveals the difficult epistemological questions surrounding personal writing for academic purposes and about teaching it to our students. These questions—and my attempts to answer them—will be explored at length in the next several chapters. Ultimately, because there are useful ways to address these concerns and because the overlapping of experiential and academic perspectives promises a richer understanding of a topic, I press for personal experience as evidence in academic argument.

(Not) Choosing Sides

Thinking about the definitions, debates, and limits of using personal experience as evidence helps me as I consider my response to Michelle's draft. I could seize upon her insights about her family and say, "Tell me more about this family and what you see when you turn homeward in your writing" (which I do say, of course, but not only that). I could say, "Forget your struggle with these tough essays by Erdrich and Dillard. You are a developing writer; it's enough that your writer's voice rings so loud and clear in the personal paragraphs" (but, of course, voice alone is not enough for first-year composition students nor for any academic writer). I do not want

Michelle to embrace the personal at the expense of learning how to write academic discourse in its broadest sense. The logic and evidential tradition of academic discourse as it is regularly composed in our field today plays an important role in clarifying and extending disciplinary conversations. Neither do I wish to sustain disciplinary binaries, for I agree with Villanueva that

> [w]e must remain conscious of tendencies to polarize, continue to refigure our notions of voice and autobiography, separate the notion of authenticity from writing about the self (or at least as the exclusive property of writing about the self), separate writing about the self from hierarchical notions of genres. ("Personal" 52)

Discussing Paulo Freire's work, Villanueva offers one way of thinking about how theoretical and experiential frameworks work together. He speaks about a Freirian dialectic between experience and theory, which involves "generalizing, theorizing, and questioning the systemic based on the personal" (*Bootstraps* xvii). According to Villanueva, his critical autobiography, *Bootstraps,* follows this dialectical principle. It attempts "to provide a problematic based on sets of experience: an experience which leads to a theory, a theory that recalls an experience; reflections on speculations, speculations to polemics to reflections" (*Bootstraps* xvii). We are beginning to see more evidence of the kind of writing Villanueva argues for—the blurred genre of personal academic argument—and because we are seeing it, on occasion, in our own journals and books, I can more readily teach it to Michelle.

But concerns remain and objections go unanswered, and as a result, I go to conferences where I use the words *personal essay* and all matter of discussion ensues that has nothing to do with what I am trying to say but is a response from those who would choose *only* personal writing *or* academic discourse. It seems to me that if I am to adequately guide Michelle and the rest of my students to fashion an argument of personal academic materials, I will need to acknowledge these concerns and provide responses to worthy objections. At the same time, I will need to offer those who already favor personal writing a clearer conception of its "work" as academic discourse, so that they can decide how it may best be used. This book is my effort to demonstrate the serious scholarly project that is personal academic writing.

2 / The Personal Is Rhetorical

Pointing to Michelle's single experiential paragraph nested within her academic essay, I ask, "Why did you decide to include this discussion of your family right here?" Michelle is worried. She thinks that she has committed some breach of composition etiquette. "We're not allowed to do that, right?" she speaks into my desk. "But it just seemed like we, my parents, do just what these authors, Dillard and Erdrich, say we should, except not as much. I don't know. It just seemed to fit. But I know that we aren't supposed to be writing about ourselves. I'll just take that out, okay?" Michelle's response does not surprise me. At the start of each fall semester, my first-year writing students and I spend some class time listing taboos associated with "school" writing. Although I have yet to find a student who can explain why she or he believes it to be the case, invariably, my developing writers tell me that the pronoun *I* should never be used in essays, in reports, or in something they call "compositions."

Over the years, I have encountered all manner of convoluted attempts to produce prose free of the recalcitrant *I* (a particularly tricky feat when trying to write about oneself). Often, what students take to be injunctions against the first-person pronoun are actually cautionaries about redundant structures, like "I think" or "I believe," or expressions of emotional response when analytic or informational discourse is called for. Most college writing teachers seem to have a fairly expansive appreciation of self-reference ("Yes, Jan, it's clear that you 'believe' that 'news media influence young people' because *you* wrote the argument"), as well as some tolerance for a student's misreading the requirements for the assignment ("No, Chris, the fact that you cried when you read 'Barn Burning' doesn't tell us about Faulkner's depiction of social hierarchies").

But *the personal* at the center of composition debates is of a different character and magnitude entirely. This *personal* involves a particular way of conveying information that seems to represent an autonomous writer's unmediated reflection on his or her "authentic" lived experience. For many compositionists, personal student writing presumes, or at least implies, a unified subject unfettered by social arrangements, history, or language. This is the personal of controversy, a personal that sets off alarms wherever it appears in student prose.

Subject formation is thus a central philosophical question that makes it difficult to move beyond one particular conception of personal writing. For many compositionists, *the personal* signifies not simply a genre of writing nor even a set of discursive strategies but an epistemological category. *The personal* opposes *the social*, which designates both the apparatus of politics, language, and conventions and the elements of everyday living that occur outside one's immediate circle. A social life appears to be more voluntary and also more material than a personal life, which may be entirely cerebral or may involve activities or contacts unknown to most of one's social acquaintances. *The personal* signals an identity, a seemingly essential set of attributes and behaviors that can be marked off as separate from others. Because such notions of the personal are both invisible and indelible, writing theorists and teachers are rightfully cautious about encouraging students to invoke their experiences.

It seems to me that reactions to the personal (pro and con) are often automatic and quite shrill, but they suggest that both those who exploit and those who oppose personal writing insist on its status as an epistemological category. In this chapter, I want to take a long look at the category of the personal, to detach it (at least partially) from its epistemological underpinnings, so that it might be understood as a rhetorically forceful construct. I begin with current conceptions of experiential discourses, which derive from enduring distinctions between mind and body, as well as from political and social contexts. While we must acknowledge that material conditions are both the cause and effect of particular subject constructions, I argue that defining personal discourse *only* in situational terms may limit its rhetorical (and therefore political) force. Feminist rhetorical theory helps me to read closely Lillian Bridwell-Bowles's personal academic essay, to establish the political weight the rhetorical personal can wield. Addressing the problem of the personal for postmodern notions of subjectivity, I use excerpts from published and student essays to explain how we might reconceive personal subjectivity as a rhetorical construct. Narrative and essay theory helps me to argue that writing the personal is a rhetorical act, as illustrated in Alice Walker's "Beyond the Peacock." Her essay manages ethical appeal while reaffirming the fragmented, deconstructed subject. Rhetorically purposeful personal writing like Walker's creates a convincing, complex, theoretically satisfying argument that foregrounds, in Kenneth Burke's sense, simultaneous identification and difference among readers and writers.

The Politics of the Personal

To appreciate the controversy over personal writing in composition studies, we need to understand how the category of the personal has traditionally been understood. By emphasizing the politics of the personal at the start of my discussion, I hope to expose the ways in which self-referential writing has been defined by dualisms. By viewing the personal rhetorically rather than epistemologically, we can begin to uncouple these artificial binaries and strengthen the potential of experience-based writing for making worthy arguments. In the discussion below, I use the term *politics* in two ways: first, to mark publicly and legally sanctioned efforts to segregate and marginalize a range of topics and issues from public discourse and concern and, second, to signify the uses to which personal writing has been put in order to overcome such hierarchies.

In popular discourse, *personal* is often synonymous with *private,* a category sustained by custom and law as outside public purview and interference. In America, reluctance or refusal to disclose on the grounds that certain sentiments or events are "too personal"

is socially appropriate behavior, and in this way, the personal affili-
ates with convention and taboo. As Nancy Fraser points out, because
the categories "public" and "private" have political power, the personal is politically implicated. Fraser shows that the private concept
"domestic violence" became a public concern when feminists were
able to muster the discursive forces to publicize and sensitize people
to its ubiquity. Hence, the terms *private* and *public*

> are not simply straightforward designations of societal
> spheres; they are cultural classifications and rhetorical la-
> bels. In political discourse, they are powerful terms that are
> frequently deployed to delegitimate some interests, views,
> and topics and to valorize others. (Fraser 21–22)

As feminists have demonstrated, erasing divisions that keep private
experience from public scrutiny and critique demands not simply
new legislation but, more significantly, changes in social etiquette
and discursive propriety.

Unfortunately, grounded as they are in Western philosophy and
tradition, artificial distinctions tend to endure. The mind-body
dualism, which traditionally associated reason with the male sphere
and emotion, body, and nature with the female sphere, has long
unsettled the realm of personal experience. Tracing the dualisms
attached to masculine and feminine consciousness from ancient to
contemporary times, Lynn Sukenick suggests that the attribution of
intuition and sensibility to female knowing, associated with women's
immediate relationship to their surroundings and to their biology
(in place of logic and detached analysis), relegates lived experience
to its own subordinate domain (40).

Recently, however, social theorists, prompted by feminist
thought, have begun to reexamine the assumptions about the body's
effect on the mind. In philosophy, Mark Johnson argues that the
metaphors we use to make sense of the world begin with the body
and its orientation and are carried "forward" to mental images of
related concepts. According to Johnson, our worldviews or ways of
understanding involve not just our intellectual, social, and cultural

affects but our physical ones as well. In fields as wide-ranging as anthropology, medicine, language philosophy, sociology, and cultural studies, researchers are now arguing for the significant impact of the quintessential personal: the effect of the body, both materially and socially constructed, on the mind.

Such disciplinary efforts admirably attempt to reorient contemporary epistemology to the physical and experiential. Still, without interrogating the binary itself, the privileging of mind over body, instead of the other way around, leaves intact a particular way of reading the world. As feminist critics have long recognized, a mere reversal of hierarchical thinking will not resolve social injustice. In fact, as early as 1977, Sukenick warned that privileging intuition over intellect places women, and particularly women writers, in the double bind of having to choose between celebrating their inherent sensibility, which ultimately leads to their silence, or repudiating the value of the so-called "feminine" qualities in favor of a "masculinist" rationality. More recent feminists have launched similar warnings, not only about the trap of making claims to women's difference that will ultimately perpetuate marginalization and limit agency but also about the danger of reading women's differences as a monocultural category (Brady).

For years, feminists have worked to turn the notion that "the personal is political" into a commonplace. They have helped to make socially marginalized arenas, such as home, family, relationships, and caregiving, matters that demand public scrutiny and legislative intervention. Likewise, feminists have used experiential discourse to subvert traditional discourses that sustain hierarchies and hide ideological agendas. However, while feminists have helped to legitimate experiential evidence as few others have, the personal is not *women's* writing. Joy Ritchie and Kate Ronald explain that both public and private argument have been integral to women's rhetorical history and that

> to see argument as male and narrative as female, for example, or to locate patriarchal discursive authority in the rational mind and feminist authority in subjective experience—not

only may be inaccurate but also may limit women's rhetorical options and ignore the rhetorical power of much of women's writing throughout history. (234–35)

Furthermore, as I suggested earlier, gendering discourse seems reductive and, ultimately, unhelpful. Rather than designating personal writing as *simply* about individuals or particular groups, we need to interrogate how it functions to effect change and why it succeeds as political work.

Personal Political Rhetoric: A Model

That the personal can be subversive is enough reason for some compositionists, both male and female, to experiment with varied, alternative points of view in their writing and teaching. But the political power of such writing also requires an awareness that discourse is conditioned by a writer's social (including race, gender, class, religion, sexual preference) categories and position(ing)s. A "politics of location," a term coined by Adrienne Rich, is crucial to any rhetoric that invokes personal experience and offers personal disclosure. It involves, according to Rich, "[r]ecognizing our location, having to name the ground we're coming from, the conditions we have taken for granted" so that we may "take responsibility" for these conditions and their effects on (especially the oppression of) others ("Notes" 219).

Discussing a theory of location for ethnographic composition research, Gesa E. Kirsch and Joy S. Ritchie explain that Rich is asking women to "investigate what has shaped their own perspectives and acknowledge what is contradictory, and perhaps unknowable, in that experience" (9). In Kirsch and Ritchie's reading of Rich, a politics of location means that "theorizing begins with the material, not transcending the personal, but claiming it" (7), and they urge that compositionists "theorize their locations by examining their experiences as reflections of ideology and culture, by reinterpreting their experiences through the eyes of others, and by recognizing their own split selves, their multiple and often unknowable identities" (8).[1]

Lillian Bridwell-Bowles's "Freedom, Form, Function: Varieties of Academic Discourse" reveals how such goals might be accomplished, providing an exemplar of experienced-based writing that self-consciously attends to both narrator's and audience's complex locations as it engages in serious political work. Published in 1995, Bridwell-Bowles's *CCC* article argues for equipping students to use writing to imagine alternative scenarios, "to think outside the boundaries of the familiar" for positive social (by way of educational and intellectual) transformation (59). In her essay, Bridwell-Bowles offers "some details from my personal history [to] explain why I care about these issues" (47). Consistent with feminist practice, the narrative portion of her essay begins by acknowledging her social "location"—a relatively privileged childhood—and admits the limits of that particular perspective.

> I was born in 1947, and promptly named "Lilly," which was extremely appropriate, given the nature of my middle class, lily-white surroundings in central Florida. Our neighborhood was typical of many built by those seeking to forget what they had experienced during the Great Depression and World War II. Our home was my father's "castle" and my mother was the superwoman who ran it and orchestrated the lives of the children she considered "gifted." (47)

As CCCC chair, Bridwell-Bowles wants her argument to appeal to a diverse group of readers, and personal references enable her to acknowledge both difference and commonalty:

> My experience in this profession will resonate with some of you, particularly those who were in school during the late sixties or early seventies. Others will have had entirely different experiences, and you will agree or disagree with me for your own reasons. (47)

By self-consciously claiming her position from the start, she can acknowledge among audience members differences in race, class, and gender. While restricting her right to speak *for* or speak *as*, such acknowledgment permits her to speak *to* her diverse group of listeners (and readers) about the importance of multiple perspectives. Following feminist bell hooks and others, Bridwell-Bowles states "how very important it is to position oneself clearly with one's listeners or readers, especially when the subject is complicated" (47). The listener or reader then has an opportunity to judge the speaker or writer by understanding who she is and where she comes from.

In an essay that invokes "the power of communication to change things, to transform" (47), Bridwell-Bowles sets the stage for representing such change within her own racially circumscribed experience by defining racial intolerance and conflict in her family and neighborhood.

> Our world was fairly homogenized, as were many in the 1950s. I recall hearing murmurs in the neighborhood when a Cuban doctor bought a house during the first wave of Cuban immigration before Castro's revolution. He was very "light skinned," they said, and welcome, of course, but no one invited him or his family to dinner. I had to travel to North Carolina to my grandparents' homes to actually meet any people of color whose names and histories were accessible to me. There, as a small child, I saw my father's hand remain at his side when a friend from his childhood extended his hand in friendship, a hand that happened to be black. This act, which is indelibly recorded in my memory, made no sense to me, coming as I did from that lily-white world where white hands clasped in greeting all the time. (47–48)

In this way, Bridwell-Bowles's account presents a determined effort to disclose her family's biases, to offer an opportunity for readers to "calibrate the sinuous relations between the life and the work in each case," by attempting to "reach a useful understanding of a scholar's life and work and a concomitant understanding of how *that* understanding affects our assessment of the value of scholarship"

(Bérubé 1067, emphasis in original). Moreover, it registers the child's disconnection from her community's values, emphasizing that such disturbances mark "the gaps" in our understanding where change becomes possible (Bridwell-Bowles 50). This gap widens further in the next paragraph as Bridwell-Bowles interrupts her narrative to mention her surprise, while reading a book by Zora Neale Hurston, to realize that the community Hurston describes was only a few miles from her home. Literally locating her early experiences geographically and socioeconomically by means of contrast to other locations allows Bridwell-Bowles to credibly advocate the efficacy of "multiple identities, multiple languages, and multiple rhetorics" (54).

Because Bridwell-Bowles wants to argue that writing classrooms can be important sites for initiating social change, she arranges much of her autobiographical material into a literacy narrative, charting her writing and reading experiences, her reproduction of traditional academic forms and the attendant limits to her understanding of "the power of the written word to change anything" (48). In this way, she allies herself with many of our students who, in 1994 and even today, hold steadfast to old, safe discursive models but who might nonetheless learn to write and to read and to "imagine something different, to see things in a new way . . . to imagine . . . what the changes ought to be" (59). As a youngster, Bridwell-Bowles found that her reading and writing outside the classroom offered alternative discourses and perspectives, and it is these multiple understandings and multiple (conflicted) identities she models as she urges teachers of composition to engender in themselves and encourage in their students alternatives to academic discourse, "writing that is not always about later, about jobs and careers" (51).

In "Freedom, Form, Function," the personal "locates" Bridwell-Bowles in the past and present. Subsequent personal disclosures, which on occasion interrupt the essay's remaining exposition and argument, continue to define and confirm the writer's own disunity, subjectivity, complexity, and multiplicity. What is constant within this representation is a self-reflective narrator, necessarily self-conscious of her tenuous position and, therefore, given the particular setting and audience, more likely to receive a hearing. Bridwell-Bowles's stories construct an argument that refuses both identity politics and "hopeless relativism" (58). Her personal account offers a model of changing perspectives and establishes an experience-bound "location" from which readers and writer might come to agree or disagree.

Although practiced writing teachers may find that personal writing offers strategies for helping students subvert traditional modes and expectations in order to accomplish serious political projects, new teachers and graduate students may believe that political motives are not sufficient justification for introducing blurred genres or experienced-based writing into their classrooms. They may, in fact, decide to assign personal narratives because they believe such essays are "easy" to write or, in contrast, they may decree self-reference too soft, too emotive to be part of first-year composition instruction. Taking either of these positions at face value, however, overlooks the theory at the center of one's pedagogical decisions. To realize the possibilities of personal writing for making academic arguments, writing instructors need to meet head on epistemological concerns about what the category of the personal means. In the next section, I examine further the vexed question of the postmodern subject in order to move a pace beyond it and into the domain of rhetoric.

The Construct of the Personal Subject

Postmodernist problems with the personal stem from its representation of the self as an inviolate and coherent human core, a self whose observations and feelings are incontrovertible and uncontested by virtue of their essentiality. Postmodernists question this view of the self and what it suggests about human agency. Certainly, it is difficult today to think of a self in autonomous terms without recognizing immediately the effects of ideology and language in a self's construction. Likewise, since we are always standing in multiple subject positions and are hailed in multiple, contradictory ways, we try to avoid misreading the personal as an individual's wholeness, unity, or plenitude. We recognize that individuals are fragmented and fragmentary. In fact, theorists today use the word *subject* rather than *individual* to emphasize the formations that "subject," or structure, human identity and thinking.[2]

While this contemporary perspective on the subject is hard to deny, it imposes difficulties for feminist theorists, who recognize, as do members of other marginalized groups, that identity and agency are requisite to enacting social change. Questioning the powerlessness of the culturally determined postmodern subject, feminists seek to construct a collective subject whose experience is neither representative of nor assumed to speak for all women. Susan Jarratt explains that feminist rhetoric moves beyond and through rhetoric's acknowledged persuasive forces to identify the "specificity and materiality of difference" ("Introduction" 9).[3] Feminist rhetoric is thus a process of articulating differences and exposing power implicit in these differences while naming connections within their historically bound contexts. The feminist subject remains fragmented, multiple, and unreconciled, yet it is a subject for whom some action is possible because of the agency of rhetoric.[4]

In the face of feminist and postmodernist conceptions of the fragmented, socially constructed subject, the personal of composition instruction becomes problematic if it represents a stable and unmediated mind at work. (For compositionists who understand the power of discourse to promote change, it is equally problematic if the writer is so deconstructed that action is impossible.) For many composition theorists, the specific genre of the personal essay seems to be especially misleading, fostering a naive, ideologically imbued individualism (Bartholomae; France)[5] that allows us to "forget" our own subjected status and to imagine that we can write within an ideologically free space. Even those who advocate personal writing assert that personal essays seem to provide a particularly inviting escape (France; Haefner; Atkins; Elbow, "Reflections"; Hesse, "Essays and Experience").

By examining the rhetorical moves in personal essays, however, we may come to understand and respond to concerns about subjectivity and agency in personal accounts, and thus we may be more likely to admit personal experience into our repertoire for academic arguments. In a traditional reading of an essay, we will most likely discern a coherent, autonomous "individual" point of view if we attribute to the writer the characteristics of the narrator. Essayists themselves deliberately encourage this kind of (mis)reading, which is consistent with the way readers typically approach fiction prose. Thus, Carl H. Klaus writes

> As the essayists see it, then, the essay, far from being a form of nonfiction, is a profoundly fictive kind of writing. It seeks to convey the sense of human presence, a human presence that is indisputably related to its author's deepest sense of self, but that is also a complex illusion of that self. ("Essayists" 173)[6]

To deepen our understanding of the distinction between essayists and narrators of essays, we can turn to Wayne C. Booth's discussion of the so-called real author, the implied author, and the narrator in fictive texts. Just as the novelist constructs within the text an implied author, the "best version" of himself or herself, representing the "character" of the author that readers will discern, so too the implied essayist is "always distinct from the 'real man'— whatever we may take him to be" (Booth 151). Booth stipulates that the implied author is not the same as the novel's narrator, who tells about (and sometimes participates in) the novel's action or sequence of events.[7] Extending Booth's rubrics, Seymour Chatman explains that within every text is "an inscribed principle of invention and intent," which Chatman refers to as the "implied author[,] . . . the reader's source of instruction about how to read the text and how to account for the selection and ordering of its components" (*Coming* 83–84). This notion of an implied author reminds us that even in essays, at the moment of publication, the writer steps away from the text, leaving readers to construct the essayist through their engagement with the work.

Essayists often admit their complicity in creating various narrative personas to meet the needs of particular essays. Scott Russell

Sanders asserts, "The first person singular is too narrow a gate for the whole writer to pass through. What we meet on the page is not the flesh-and-blood author but a simulacrum, a character who wears the label *I*" (39–40). Sanders also notes that in her introduction to *A Room of One's Own*, Virginia Woolf declares the narrator, the "I" who speaks in her essay, "only a convenient term for somebody who has no real being. Lies will flow from my lips," Woolf asserts, "but there may perhaps be some truth mixed up with them; it is for you to seek out this truth and to decide whether any part of it is worth keeping" (4; qtd. in Sanders 40). Likewise, E. B. White confesses that "the essayist arises in the morning and, if he has work to do, selects his garb from an unusually extensive wardrobe: he can pull on any sort of shirt, be any sort of person, according to his mood or his subject matter" ("Foreword" vii). Such admissions confirm that like fiction, nonfiction writing features a multiplicity of representations.

These writers likewise acknowledge the impossibility of accessing through writing some kind of return to an authentic "inner person." As such, Roland Barthes makes explicit the fragmented, constructed self of autobiographical writing when he writes in his experimental memoir,

> I do not strive to put my present expression in the service of my previous truth (in the classical system, such an effort would have been sanctified under the name of *authenticity*), I abandon the exhausting pursuit of an old piece of myself, I do not try to *restore* myself (as we say of a monument). I do not say: "I am going to describe myself" but: "I am writing a text, and I call it R. B." I shift from imitation (from description) and entrust myself to nomination. Do I not know that, *in the field of the subject, there is no referent*? (56)

Throughout his book *Roland Barthes by Roland Barthes*, the writer calls attention to the fictive, socially constructed, socially mediated nature of both personal experience and the first-person narrator who represents that experience.

Emphasizing the reader's significant participation in constructing a fictive text, Douglas Hesse speculates that the popularity of personal writing comes from the desire for orderly existence, although he emphasizes that the form of the essay, not the agent narrator, provides the appearance of order. Describing "the enabling fiction of the autonomous essayist rendering personal truths," Hesse explains that

> essayists display knowledge as entailed by experience; [but] when readers extend "truths" beyond the text, they reveal their own desire for order. . . . As a consequence, we should view personal or familiar or exploratory essays not as presented artifacts but as emplotted experiences, persuading by storying propositions into their readers' experiences. ("Essays and Experience" 210–11)

Accepting (or rejecting) the narrator's representation of self and experience is a convention for reading essays, akin to "the willing suspension of disbelief" for reading fiction. It is a choice made by readers who, according to Hesse, embrace the illusion of textual stability. Personal reference can thus be understood as strategically oriented toward masking the separation between the narrator and essayist for the benefit of *both* writer and audience. Fashioning a unified, authentic, and worthy "self," the essayist sustains the illusion of coherence by exploiting ethical appeal, a persuasive strategy reaching back to the classical tradition. In *On Rhetoric*, Aristotle recognizes the persuasive force of character, "for we believe fair-minded people to a greater extent and more quickly [than we do others] on all subjects in general and completely so in cases where there is not exact knowledge but room for doubt" (1.2.4). According to Aristotle's instructions, the persuasive speaker will be the kind of person who inspires confidence because he or she possesses practical wisdom, virtue, and good will toward the listening audience.

We can gather a sense of how compositionists use character in academic discourse by looking at Laurie Grobman's "Just Multiculturalism," an argument for replacing the key term *tolerance* with *justice* in theorizing multicultural debates over moral relativism. My comments regarding Grobman's essay are not meant to suggest that such strategies are reserved for writing professionals. On the contrary, I encourage instructors to teach students to similarly identify and use their experiences to construct persuasive personal appeals. In her essay, Grobman invokes the personal to establish her scholarly and moral credibility. At one point, she interrupts her largely abstractive commentary and scholarly analysis to assess the values she wishes to pass on to her two young children:

> I am certain that I want them to have an historical aware-ness of the valuable contributions diverse cultures and people have made to our world, as well as the ways many minority and non-Western cultures have been systemati-cally undervalued, marginalized, and oppressed. I also want them to use critical judgment fairly and consistently, and not tolerate difference for difference's sake. ("Just" 840)

By framing her argument about the need not simply to talk about but also to act in terms of values she wishes to impart to her children, Grobman highlights her own deliberate choices and attributes of character and establishes herself as a tolerant and just human being, one who is justified in carrying on this particular argument.

Furthermore, by personalizing the conflicts and revealing her desire to see justice enacted in the face of obstacles created by hyper-theorizing, Grobman invites multicultural scholars, who may feel themselves caught between social construction and foundationalism, to share her ethos. Asking whether "we [have] lost sight of the im-portant cultural work of multiculturalism," Grobman asserts,

> I will continue the intellectual work of asserting compel-ling principles in the face of what may seem like an intel-lectual maze with no way out. I want to move in the direc-tion of articulating and clarifying principles of justice, and basing the work of multiculturalism on them. In advocat-ing this position, I acknowledge that I may be caught in the

trap of my culturally encoded perspectives but have chosen not to be hamstrung by this Catch-22. ("Just" 840)

Here personal disclosures are especially strategic, for Grobman is a
white multiculturalist and hence subject to suspicion by some in her
discipline. She establishes her authority by revealing her knowledge
of the disciplinary debates and her right to speak by revealing herself as an invested human being, admitting her socially constructed
location but refusing to concede to its limitations. Grobman then
turns up the emotional pitch by way of a brief personal narrative.
The discourse shifts from academic argument to a story about the
writer's child, culminating with a pun on *just,* the contested term
in Grobman's analysis.

Recently, my younger son came home from school and
began telling me what he had learned about Rosa Parks and
Martin Luther King, Jr. He asked me, with genuine sincer-
ity as well as disbelief, "Mommy, how could people be so
mean just because of darker skin?" Before I could answer,
he declared, "I would never do that," and then went out to
play. In the end, it is *just* that simple. ("Just" 840–41)

Invoking her son's guileless question, Grobman relies on the
audience's concordant beliefs not only in the need for greater social
justice but also that it can be taught, must be taught, despite our
recognition of theoretical ambiguities and political contradictions.
Thus Grobman's experiential evidence contributes to her credibility, heightens the emotional pitch of her argument, and secures her
audience's intellectual investment and social commitment.

Once again, I want to stress that the narrator of Grobman's essay is and is not the same person who occupies an office down the
hall from mine. As readers, we assume that nonfiction reflects the
values of its writer (and in this case, it does, but that's not what is
important here). But we do not reproduce ourselves in writing;
rather, as Aristotle suggests, we select strategically the most appropriate versions and representations to complete our rhetorical pur-

poses, while acknowledging as postmodern thinkers our inability to access a stable, singular psychic core. This is not an incidental point for our students to understand about the essays they read and to exploit in their own writing.

Constructing the Subject in/of Student Writing

Although the illusion of essayistic coherence is appealing, we can help students to appreciate that they will not discover the "true" individual hidden under the narrator's (or writer's) mantle. In the *Rhetoric*, Aristotle emphasizes the audience's perception of the orator, pointing out that ethos "should result from the speech, not from a previous opinion that the speaker is a certain kind of person" (1.2.4). He states that it is necessary "that the speaker *seem* to be a certain kind of person and that his hearers *suppose* him to be disposed toward them in a certain way . . . A person *seeming* to have all these qualities is necessarily persuasive to the hearers" (2.1.2, 6, emphasis added). These comments, which have caused so much debate among scholars, seem to invite the speaker to develop an impressive persona or literary mask to sway the audience.[8] At the same time, I do not mean to suggest that the writer's many "selves" or the narrative roles he or she might assume are merely an assembly of cloaks that may be elected or rejected at will, nor do I want to lose sight of the linguistic preconditions that construct a writer's thinking.[9]

The complexities of narrative subjectivity are illustrated in "Subverting Ideologies and Understanding Racism," an essay written by Devin, a college junior majoring in professional writing. In his ongoing, self-reflective project, Devin, a white student, reveals the struggle to perform a subject position in an essay in which the writer himself tries to understand and express his socially subjected status, as well as to acknowledge his role in and to redeem himself for perpetuating social injustice. Devin's polemical, mixed-genre essay was "performed" in his theater studies course for the only African American teacher on campus; it calls for a redefinition of governmental and individual responses to racism based upon an attitude of empathy rather than a notion of tolerance.

In the lengthy personal narrative that forms the essay's first major section, Devin's narrator establishes his "right" to criticize those whom he holds responsible for fostering and sustaining racism and oppression: the U.S. legal apparatus, from law enforcement to the courts. He describes his parents as "racist, though they undoubtedly perceive themselves differently" and his high school as "a predominately white school full of racist ideology," where the administration handles racial conflicts among students by forbidding "hats, baggy jeans, and other wardrobe that could be considered offensive" in a move to "ban the culture, not address the problem." Devin's introduction centers on his friendship with Charles, a young African American man who, like Devin, is a "part-time father" and who shared with Devin "personal histories of poverty and a sense of alienation from organized society."

The narrator of the text tries to find a place for himself in the world (and in the text) by marking out his relation to and his relations with his African American friend and their location in the inner city. He repeatedly identifies himself with Charles: his appreciation for Charles's music, Charles's pals, Charles's community, and the comfort he finds in watching their two sons' easy play. He wants his readers to know that despite their racial differences, he and Charles are very much alike, as the theme of identification is central to his suasive project. Thus he takes great pains to establish a credible ethos: he is reflective ("I begin to feel a sense of guilt that seemed to be lacking in my classmates, a racial guilt"); he is intelligent ("I do not want to say that we were colorblind; anyone who advocates colorblind relationships also advocates discounting of cultural connections and feelings"); he is principled ("I refused to pay the fine for 'missing a stop sign' because I felt so strongly that the police had racially profiled Charles and I").

At the same time, he carefully undermines traditional notions of what an individual of "good character" should be. For example, he writes, "One night Charles and I were about to make a drug run into [the urban center] . . . when my tire blew out," jarringly asserting an "alternative" dimension of his daily life. Later in the essay, he recounts a scene of police harassment during which the local police flashed their lights behind them and "[p]anic streamed through us as we quickly hid our drug paraphernalia throughout the car." Devin goes on to claim that he "had been stopped by police too many times not to notice patterns in the typical lines of argument" and that their subsequent search for weapons and drugs (as opposed to alcohol, the supposed substance of choice for Irishmen like him) was a case of racial profiling. He states, "The assumption that 'probable cause' was established for a drug search could have no other root than the ideology that blacks are drug users and 'gang bangers.'" In fact, he was so outraged that he refused to pay the fine on his traffic violation and was ultimately sentenced to two days in prison. In this essay, then, the narrator is a kind of antihero who invites us to accept and to doubt his credibility for, at least as Devin constructs his story, he and Charles were using drugs (if not at that moment, then often enough to be carrying drugs and drug paraphernalia in their car). Devin subverts traditional views of the "good white boy" by announcing his guilt and identifying himself with something he views as outside the purview of white experience, a gesture that he feels will build his credibility by giving him an insider's edge.

I like this essay as much for what it gives away as for what it says. Devin wants to persuade his audience that racism is wrong and that the history of the United States bears witness to this country's political and legislative support for racial oppression. In the second part of his essay, he traces out a history of slavery, legal sanctions against African Americans, and resultant intolerance for racial or cultural difference. While his personal narrative reflects identification with the Other, the exposition reveals the culpability of all (including Devin) who enjoy what he terms "white privilege." He makes these arguments either because he thinks his audience needs convincing or because he believes that his audience needs to know that Devin himself has been enlightened. When I first read Devin's essay, I assumed he was imagining an academic readership (since he'd told me he wanted to submit his article for publication). If that were the case, I thought, he had somehow failed to discern the liberatory agenda of much of the scholarly community and was, in effect, "preaching to the converted." Later, I realized that Devin was writing for his high school classmates and teachers, his parents, and the people in his hometown, all those whom he felt needed a more enlightened worldview. For this audience, his fragmented, generous, antihero was the appropriate rhetorical choice.

Devin's essay also illustrates Mikhail Bakhtin's point that subject construction is an ongoing process of intersections among discursive formations. In *The Dialogic Imagination*, Bakhtin explains that while our language, and thus our way of thinking, strives toward a single, unitary expression, it is simultaneously stratified by competing social and historical discourses that fill each word with a multitude of prior associated meanings. The individual consciousness evolves in a struggle among the words of authority (externally authoritative discourse, which is held fairly stable), the words of others (internally persuasive discourse), and our own words. "The importance of struggling with another's discourse, its influence in the history of an individual's coming to ideological consciousness is enormous," Bakhtin states. "One's own discourses and one's own voice, although born of another or dynamically stimulated by another, will sooner or later begin to liberate themselves from the authority of the other's discourse" (348).[10] In other words, Devin's essay constructs a particular subjectivity, one influenced by and constituted through the clash of discursive authorities, among them his family's and community's values, his conversations with Charles, his engagement with college texts, and his theater arts professor's responses to his essay drafts.

But the self of this essay is not more or less authentic than the selves of other essays that Devin writes, nor is it unitary. Barbara Kamler, among others, has argued that a writer's subjectivity is rewritten and relocated in literacy practices (50).[11] Writing is a transformative activity that calls into play "historically and culturally received patterns of meaning" (54). In Devin's case, his use of historical research, his inclusion of contemporary authors like Richard Rodriguez, his understanding of racism and how it might be described or contested textually, and his sense of how to present an argument that is acceptable to his audience provide multiple perspectives that confirm and contradict each other. At the same time, in "the process of making and remaking" (54), the transformative activity of writing not only reconstructs the text but likewise reconstructs the writer as he or she composes. As Devin represents his experiences semiotically, he focuses, refines, and reconceptualizes the relations among his engagement with Charles, his encounters with law enforcement agencies, his felt obligation to his young son, and his reading of prior texts. These reciprocal readings and writings will ultimately change the meaning of the story he is creating, giving greater scope to Devin's understanding, as well as to his rhetorical repertoire.

Rhetorical Agency in Personal Essays

In this chapter, I have highlighted scholarly and student essays, texts used mainly for academic purposes. In these cases, personal references can be considered atypical or, as I have said, controversial. In contrast, nonacademic essays have a long tradition of using personal experience to make and prove arguments, yet personal narratives are the genre of greatest concern to social constructionists in composition.[12] For these reasons, I turn now to Alice Walker's "Beyond the Peacock: The Reconstruction of Flannery O'Connor." By interrogating the relationship between the essay's writer construct and its rhetorical agency, I hope to reaffirm the efficacy of personal appeals. If we acknowledge that every writing is, to a greater or lesser extent, a rhetorical *performance*, we will begin to see that a writer's inferred authenticity and wholeness may be irrelevant to the agency of the rhetorical personal. If we grant that personal narratives make convincing arguments, we will more likely appreciate this genre as a starting point for other kinds of writing.

"Beyond the Peacock," an essay that foregrounds divided loyalties, fragmented subjectivity, and cultural conflict, is especially appropriate for this analysis. It centers on Alice Walker's 1974 trip to Milledgeville, Georgia. Accompanied by her mother, the narrator sets out to inspect the homes (and thus the lives) of Flannery O'Connor and her own family. The geographical tension arches between Andalusia, the country estate where O'Connor wrote until her death in 1964, and the Walker family's share-cropping farm site, where Walker had spent a year in her early childhood, only half the house still standing in the midst of a field. The thematic tension arises from the writer's ambivalence about history, literary icons, and her own place as an African American writer. While more than half the essay narrates events, observations, and conversation between Walker and her mother, other sections provide lengthy exposition: first, brief biographical information about O'Connor; then, a critical assessment of O'Connor's writing, especially its racial and racist implications.[13]

In this essay, Walker repeatedly undermines traditional assumptions about personal essays: the narrator is never unitary, and Walker emphasizes her own fragmented subjectivity. The narrator has returned to the South in search of psychological and intellectual completeness, an effort to find "a wholeness" (48), a sense of self-coherence. But her private desire links to the wider questions of history and politics. She is ever conscious of her African American history and her duty to recognize the value of that history, as well as the wrongs perpetuated by those who have traditionally recorded history. Much of her conflict results from her effort to reconcile her respect for Flannery O'Connor's writing with her obligation to resist the white Western literary canon. The narrator acknowledges O'Connor's talents; she praises O'Connor's character constructions, noting that all of her characters, regardless of race, are idiosyncratic; she finds that O'Connor's artistic development coincides with her advancing social consciousness. At the same time, she notes that elements of racism emerge in O'Connor's early stories and private letters and that O'Connor's estate represents southern white exploitation of African American labor. These dualities of knowing are dramatized as psychic conflict: looking out of the windows of a southern estate built and supported by slave labor, the narrator observes, "Between the me that is on the ground and the me that is at the windows, History is caught" (47). In this way, the narrator calls attention to the writer's ability to fill in both sides of the story.

Not only does "Beyond the Peacock" represent a destabilized, nonunitary subject, the essay likewise emphasizes that private experience is always bound up in the public and the political. In the opening scene, the narrator tells of reading her poetry at a "recently desegregated college" (42) and learning that she and O'Connor had lived in the same town; the discussion of O'Connor's writing occurs in a newly integrated hotel coffee shop, where, not coincidentally, both integration and cornbread are topics of conversational scrutiny. Observing that in the end, "It all comes back to houses. To how people live" (58), she emphasizes that the day-to-day lives of individuals and the preservation of those lives as historical artifacts are inextricably wrapped in historical, political, and social conditions.

The "Work" of the Personal

What is gained when writers of the personal like Bridwell-Bowles, Grobman, Devin, and Walker acknowledge their biases, fragmentation, and subject-construction? According to Kenneth Burke, the narrator's personal experience invites audience identification, which is always linked to persuasion (*Rhetoric* 20–23, 45–46). The personal manages this bridge in a way that no other writing can. Burkean identification generates "consubstantiality," a means of securing agreement or understanding by recognizing common interests shared between speaker and audience, writer and reader.[14]

Thus, in "Beyond the Peacock," the details of Walker's life engender shared notions of social and literary justice. She inspires identification by means of the narrative thread by which readers follow the minute details of the trip south while simultaneously drawing upon their own personal or civic experiences and their own examples of injustice. Walker's depiction of her experiences stretches the limits of this identification to propel further reflection or action.[15] As readers, we are less likely to be persuaded by the abstract and the general, which may seem ungrounded, while particulars "carry greater weight and authority" because they are associated with "experienced facts" (Anderson, *Style* 172). Grounded in experiential details (the NO TRESPASSING sign; the landlord Mr. Jenkins, whose unpaid debt stretches back to 1952; a first washing machine; the well-maintained country house; and the peacocks), readers of Walker's essay hold themselves responsible for their own "houses" and "readings." Shown the details, they cannot look away from the larger picture the details inscribe.

Significantly, appreciating the work of identification in Burke's sense of that term demands recognition of differences as well as similarities. In *A Rhetoric of Motives,* Burke declares, "[T]o begin with 'identification' is, by the same token, though roundabout, to confront the implications of *division*" (22, emphasis in original). Burke speaks of the "wavering line between identification and division" (45), noting within each term implications for its obverse, and the ease with which concepts can be manipulated toward their opposites. Nevertheless, viewing difference within identification as a rhetorical act on which both writers and readers depend can offer a corrective to essentialist and universalist readings. According to Nancy K. Miller, the feminist autobiographer

> constructs herself in language—precisely at the intersection of cultural codes about women. . . . These at least doubly-coded spaces of constructed identity in writing are, I think, what allows for readerly connection across the grain of cultural difference, crossing but not dissolving in a double movement of identification and resistance. (126)

For Miller, "resistance" marks the reader's positive response to textual invitations to "forget" difference, to universalize and thus objectify particular, lived experience.[16]

Walker's use of personal experience exploits the double-sidedness of feminist identification. "Beyond the Peacock" reveals the particularities of one woman's experience through rich descriptive detail and metareflection. While these strategies invite identification, especially at the political and social level, they likewise mark out sites of potential difference of class, race, gender, and geography between Walker and O'Connor and between the essayist and (some of) her readers. In Walker's essay, the narrator's mother evokes this rhetorical duality, inviting identification as well as recognizing division. Unwilling to allow barriers to interfere with her progress and willing to say aloud what others only think, she participates directly in the action of story, the narrator's foil and cause for conversation. The mother notices scenery different from what the narrator notices, she remembers differently, and her observations shape the narrator's memory of this trip. It is the mother who rejoices in the persistence of daffodils at the family's dilapidated farm site. In contrast to Walker's and O'Connor's concerns about representation and difference, the narrator's mother identifies with the white characters in "Everything That Rises Must Converge," a gesture that the narrator describes as "*so* Southern and *so* black" (51, emphasis in original). At the same time, the mother offers a different ending to O'Connor's story, one that entails the perspective of a contemporary African American woman. And it is the mother who has the last word in Walker's essay. In her essay "The King of the Birds," O'Connor had written, "I intend to stand firm and let the peacocks multiply, for I am sure that, in the end, the last word will be theirs" (21). Responding to the narrator's observation that O'Connor's infamous peacocks are "inspiring," her mother remarks wryly, "Yes, and they'll eat up every bloom you have, if you don't watch out" (59).

It's hard to doubt the authenticity of this mother.[17] As a character, she is so likable, so observant, yet there is something about her construction that does not ring true. Perhaps she is too much in the tradition of wise country folk, too useful to Walker's purposes, too much a contrast with the kinds of characters O'Connor's stories depict. Certainly, she is a different mother from the dignified, creative gardener described in Walker's title essay, "In Search of Our Mothers' Gardens," who, when "working in her flowers . . . is radiant, almost to the point of being invisible—except as Creator: hand and eye" (241). But "Beyond the Peacock" is an essay about historical reconstructions and an argument about our inability to tell the whole story. In shaping the experience of the mother, Walker seems to be illustrating just that point.

The Rhetorical Personal in Composition Classrooms

"No," I say to Michelle, "it's not true that you cannot talk about your family in this essay, but let's consider what you might gain by writing about them. What is the point of this essay? Where is your personal experience leading you?"

Although most of Michelle's first draft compares and cites the assigned essays, "Living Like Weasels" and "Skunk Dreams," it's obvious that she has something else on her mind. She tells me that she wants to use her essayists as sources to "prove what I was saying, to accompany my thoughts and help push them along." At one point she explains,

> With the weasel one, Dillard says, "If I could have just gone for the neck." And she's talking about if she could have just grabbed onto things and done things differently. That's when it all came together . . . about how you just, all these people wish they could have done more. That they see that other people aren't [doing more].

As Michelle begins to discuss her concerns about the insularity of contemporary suburban life, I realize that while Erdrich's and Dillard's essays seem to have stimulated her thinking, her argument derives from her observations of individuals in her own community. This is Michelle's most elaborated explanation of her intentions:

> In the last draft I was talking about how . . . people are too far from where they should be. I know that the whole thing is technology and that it's such a wonderful thing, but I think with technology and even having air conditioning and all this stuff, which is nice to have, you can step outside and enjoy the outside. . . . People think that if they have the cars and the money and the big house that it's going to make them happy, but in a lot of aspects, that's not at all what makes you happy. You can go outside and stand there and enjoy it.

A lot of people would be happier with that because the money and the houses and stuff is not what makes them happy, and I think that's what they're trying to say in the books, that you have to go outside. And people aren't experiencing things—like with the cages [the fence around the animal preserve described in "Skunk Dreams"], people are caged, and they don't get out. A lot of people from where I live in Berks County have never gotten out. They've never experienced [anything new]. They've always lived there. Some people have never traveled out of the state. And I think that's a big part of finding things you enjoy, and if you don't get out and you don't experience that, you're never gonna know what you've missed out on.

We talk at length about how she might develop her argument by staking some claims independent of the assigned readings. Michelle's next draft includes the following paragraphs:

Many people never leave the state that they live in, let alone the country, either because their lives are too busy or because they are afraid of what could happen to them while they are roaming free. Some of my best friends have never left the state of Pennsylvania. They find it completely amazing that I have lived in four other states. They gasp and say, "Wow, what is that like?" I just wonder why they haven't taken even a day trip somewhere they have never been, just to explore and see what there is to see. Traveling is a great way to experience something new and exciting. By not venturing into the great unknown, they are missing out on so much the world has to offer. I could not imagine staying in one place for my entire life. To me, it would make for a lackluster life.

My family and I make it a point to go somewhere every year. Just to get away from everything and enjoy ourselves. This "see the world mentality" comes from my parents. When they were young neither of them traveled much; it was exactly an hour's drive to the beach for my mother and her family, which is the only place they ever got to go. My father's family never took vacations because with nine children leaving the fort was just too difficult. So now that my parents are older (when most people are starting to wind down), they seem to "kick things up a bit." They take every chance they get to break free and enjoy the world and nature around them; just a trip to the flower nursery is good enough for them.

As a rhetorical strategy, Michelle's family serves as an example of "right action," in contrast to those in her community who are afraid to travel beyond the county limits. As Aristotle recommends in the *Rhetoric,* her example, drawn from real life, allows the speaker and audience to reason a general rule (the importance of travel, of seeing beyond one's immediate horizon) from particular cases (Michelle's life is not "lackluster" because her family appreciates what is gained by travel) (2.20.1–9; I will say more about Aristotle's notion of evidence by example in chapter 4). She also uses the rhetorical strategy of contrast, or demonstration from opposites, which Aristotle describes as a logical approach, useful to many kinds of arguments (2.23.1).

I find Michelle's additional paragraphs of personal experience satisfying as much for what they contribute to the development of her argument as for what they reveal about the gaps and contradictions that remain. We talk at length about the relationship between her readings and her essay's theme. She notices that Hollins Pond, the site of Dillard's weasel, is "so close to the highway; it's so close [but] people don't realize it's there." I point out that Dillard appears to be surrounded by nature, and Michelle completes my point: "She looks like she's in nature, but she's really by the highway." "So," I say, "what does this remind you of that you've already written about?" "Ah," she responds, "Going to the nursery . . . and trying to make nature out of a backyard."

Ultimately, the question is whether we are willing to allow the experiences of Dillard, Erdrich, and Michelle to coexist as evidence in the same essay on the same page. Further, we must consider what is at stake if we encourage students to make such rhetorical moves. While the politicized, cultural-critical awareness of composition justifies subverting entrenched paradigms and promoting alternative methods and alternative voices, in the end, we must realize that such instruction is both challenging and risky.

3 / Constructing Experience

Prompted by our conversation, Michelle's next draft of "Nature's Lessons" takes an interesting turn. She now complicates Dillard's and Erdrich's arguments about the inspiration of nature by contrasting the writers' stories with her family's effort to "create a nature of their own." Expanding on her discussion of the ways in which her family has attempted to "sort of make up for the nature they don't get to experience in the outdoors," she writes, "Along with the mini garden we also have azaleas, sunflowers, shrubs and miniature trees that become transplanted into our front yard. There we can sit on our porch and get away from everything and enjoy the nature that my family has created." In these sentences, Michelle purposefully opposes her family's artificially constructed natural world to the untamed, authentic wilderness, which she sees as glorified in Erdrich's and Dillard's essays. But Michelle does not capitulate to her authors' worldviews by privileging one site over the other. Her next paragraph adds a new, crucial layer to her argument.

> Our little piece of land next to the street makes us feel miles away from anywhere. Like Dillard, who appears to be surrounded by nature at Hollins Pond but she is really standing just across the road from the highway, my family and I surround ourselves with nature so that we can try to forget the world that is around us for as long as we can. We say that we are "nature people" by having these things and enjoying the outdoors, but I think, like a lot of people, we are just fooling ourselves. We don't go hiking or camping

like normal nature enthusiasts do, so it seems our nature
is just a facade, but it seems to work for us.

As a trained composition teacher, I had assumed that Michelle
would use her lived experience either to bolster the arguments of
the writers she was analyzing (in the form of additional supports)
or to argue the validity of the writers' viewpoint in contrast to "everyday" perspectives. To my surprise, Michelle does something else.
For as she considers her family's efforts to create a natural environ-
ment within their home, she raises two important questions: First,
in what ways is the re-creation of the natural world (un)achievable?
Second, is a pseudoversion of natural living better than no effort at
all? These questions, which are implied in her descriptions of family
excursions, skylights, houseplants, and mini gardens, turn Michelle's
ostensible investigation of her readings in an entirely new direction.
In this new draft, her essay moves from the theme of "what two nature writers tell us about how we should direct our lives" to a discussion of the issue of "what is possible under the circumstances."

Advocates of personal writing often remind us that when students like Michelle find connections between their lived experiences
and the texts that they read, they are more likely to master difficult
material by integrating it into familiar frameworks. For Peter Elbow,
"discourse that tries to render experience," that is, "language that con-
veys to others a sense of their [writers'] experience—or indeed, that
mirrors back to [writers] themselves a sense of their own experience
from a little distance" encourages students to write for their own
pleasure and offers an alternative approach to solving problems and
gaining new insights ("Reflections" 136–37). Elbow believes that
teaching experiential writing "help[s] students produce good academic discourse" ("Reflections" 137).

Kurt Spellmeyer makes a similar case by describing the cognitive processes of one of his first-year writing students: as an introduction to, and parallel argument for, a dilemma imposed by Jean-
Paul Sartre's existential ethical crises, the student writes about her
decision to end the life of her pet rat. Spellmeyer observes that the

student uses the devices of narrative in the same way as Sartre, "to furnish practical illustrations of philosophic principles" (274). Arguing that much academic discourse writing instruction forces students to accommodate the formal features of genre without adequate understanding of the subject matter, Spellmeyer notes that his student had "begun to perceive that the area of meaning defined by Sartre is not strictly Sartre's, or strictly her own, but a common ground" (274). By integrating her personal experience, the student had begun to internalize complex philosophic concepts. Spellmeyer predicts that if she continues to blend academic and personal discourses in her writing, "she will gradually enter the community of 'knowers' while retaining her own voice in the process" (274), because she will have a firm grasp of both content and genre. By extending Spellmeyer's observations, we come to see that Michelle's personal references initiate changes in her thinking and writing. Unlike Spellmeyer's student, who identified with her philosophic text, however, Michelle's experiences suggest contrast, contradiction, and perhaps an alternative theory.

But pointing out that Michelle's experiential account has contributed to her understanding of her readings or to her development of alternative readings and writings does not yet address the "problematic of experience" so crucial to compositionists in a postmodern world. In this chapter, I continue to explore the epistemological questions that surround experience-based writing, focusing now on *experience*, a second key term in my argument for personal experience as evidence. I examine contemporary views of experience, both as socially mediated and interpretive and as the effect of multiple reconstructions. By emphasizing the *construct* that is personal experience, I try to reduce anxiety about and, therefore, objections to invoking experience as evidence in academic writing. Linda Brodkey's essay "Writing on the Bias" helps to highlight the rhetoricity of experiential accounts, as do two student essays, which, for varying purposes, reconstruct the student writers' experiences. Having made the case for experience as representation, I complicate this issue by discussing problems caused by reading experiential evidence in this way—especially in terms of its claims to truth—and discuss two scholarly

composition texts that attempt to mediate this dilemma by emphasizing their "locations," self-constructions, contradictions, biases, and
complexities as they blend their personal accounts with academic
writing. Finally, I suggest that if students and teachers recognize and
appreciate the *construct* of experience, they can invite more complicated and more meaning-filled analysis than might be reflected
in either the personal essay or the academic argument alone.

The Construct of Experience

When a billboard on the highway near my home boasts that at our
local hospital "experience counts," or when my dear friend says,
"For my heart valve surgery, I want a doctor who does this proce-
dure routinely, someone who's performed hundreds of operations,
not one who does this once or twice a week," they are invoking the
notion of experience to suggest expertise: physicians and health
workers who have perfected their craft over years of training and
practice. In fact, we apply the same concept in reference to experienced teachers, who are often asked to mentor junior faculty. One's
experiences in this sense are supposed to lead to new and greater
knowledge, or as Aristotle argues, "We must attend, then, to the
undemonstrated remarks and beliefs of experienced and older
people or of intelligent people, no less than to demonstrations. For
these people see correctly because experience has given them their
eye" (*Nicomachean Ethics* 6.11). In other words, what we term *in-
telligence* is, in part, a consequence of experience, an appreciation
of significant particulars, as well as universals.

Experience means something quite different, however, to composition scholars. Many object to teaching personal writing because
it tends to perpetuate for students the myth of authenticity, the illusion that an individual can feel, understand, and capture in writing socially and culturally unmediated or decontextualized experience. Yet if we understand and acknowledge the interpretability and
contingency of all we name as experiential "truth," we can teach
students (and even ourselves) how to take advantage of the rhetoricity
of recorded experience.

Contemporary theory teaches us that we cannot capture in writing some "real and actual" moment in our lives. We know that every event is shaped and interpreted such that we can only speak about "how it seemed to me." If we paid careful attention, we'd see that we construct fragments of our experience into stories or mini-narratives, excluding some features and emphasizing others, to organize and make sense of them. Consistent with Hayden White's aesthetic theory of history, which recognizes that narrative form is imposed on historical events to provide a structure and thus a meaning, we tell ourselves our own personal histories by means of these self-narrated moments.[1]

Expanding White's theory to life writing, autobiographical scholar Paul John Eakin asserts,

> Whatever we know of historical reality necessarily partakes of impositions supplied by the observer, [since it is the observer who] decide[s] what constitutes an event, what is worthy of record, [based on, perhaps, unconscious] principle[s] of selection. . . . In this sense we cannot speak of 'real events' as 'offering themselves' to us ready-made, for there is no value-neutral historical reality that we can know anything about. (*Touching* 177)

James Olney defines this narrative shaping of our experiences as creating metaphors, figurative constructions that order our sense of self and the events in which this self engages. The tale of how I learned to ride a bike (my mother had given up and sent me out to the street to teach myself); the family saga of surviving my parents' divorce (I was "resilient" and didn't seem to notice); even my narrative of Michelle's development as a writer (see how much a good teacher can contribute)—all of these are stories of my own making, which have been variously shaped and colored by sundry forces.

In addition, when we read or write experienced-based discourse, we must take into account the ambiguity it suffers as a result of its various deferrals. Any conceptualization of "an experience" is already a representation of the actual event, a translation into words and interpretations the basis of which can never be re-covered.[2] We make something into an experience by ordering and arranging it as a narrative, but there is already a difference between a lived moment and our attempts to capture it in thought and words. Judith Summerfield puts it succinctly: "There is no return to the event, except 'virtually.' The event is overtaken, mediated by language. And language is always belated, always deferred, always after the event" (185). In this regard, Summerfield reminds us of the "central truths of language": that retrospection is a step removed from the event itself, that the telling moves us further away, and that understanding comes belatedly, amidst ongoing revisions (180–81).

In their own ways, essayists, autobiographers, and critical commentators insist on the same point: that memory reconstructs, rather than recreates, experience into a text, not into a truth. According to William Zinsser, "The writer of a memoir must become the editor of his or her own life, imposing a narrative pattern and an organizing idea on an unwieldy mass of half-remembered events" (13), while G. Thomas Couser observes that "memory is not a stable, static record that could ground a reliable written narrative; rather, it is itself a text under continuous unconscious revision" (17).

Moreover, we understand that the stories we tell ourselves of our experiences come filtered through the collective subjectivities of our social and cultural relationships, so that our interpretations of experience are not simply individual processes. Kenneth Burke explains that we shape our understanding of experience into

> situational patterns by means of the particular vocabulary of the cultural group into which we are born. . . . Other groups may select other relationships as meaningful. These relationships are not *realities*, they are *interpretations* of reality—hence different frameworks of interpretation will lead to different conclusions as to what reality is. (*Permanence* 35, emphasis in original)

As such, for instance, my way of experiencing the world is preconditioned by the contingencies and discourses surrounding my being born female, being born white, being a "child of divorce," being a parent, being a college writing teacher. Consistent with Burke's theory is Joan W. Scott's observation that "what *counts* as experience is neither self-evident nor straightforward; it is always contested, and always therefore political" ("Evidence" 797, my emphasis). Scott shows that experiences accrue to groups in particular ways because of the group's status or victimization, so that subjects are actually "constituted" through their experiences ("Evidence" 779; this issue is addressed in greater detail below). The work of feminist ethnographers demonstrates that knowledge of self and world is bound up with socially marked categories.[3] An appeal to experience, then, is always an interpretation, wrought through the lenses of our already constructed subjectivities.[4]

Rhetorizing Experience: A Model

Few contemporary nonfiction writers would insist that they are furnishing a "pure" account of what "actually" happened. In calling on their experiences, most writers of experience-based prose are doing something else and doing it for other purposes. Linda Brodkey's *College English* article "Writing on the Bias" illustrates how this construction works, for we can locate in Brodkey's essay the social and culture constitutions that shape not only the writer's experience but also the way she perceives or "experiences" lived events. Brodkey's essay thus provides an illustration of personal experience *as* rhetoric.

"Writing on the Bias" is an academic memoir that traces the literacy "lessons" of a working-class child who grew up to be a university English professor. In principle and practice, it is a carefully fashioned argument for alternatives to traditional scholarly discourse, and it critiques social and educational structures that sustain the veneer of objectivity in academic writing. As a contemporary writer and critic, Brodkey deliberately calls attention to the constructs and interpretations in her narrative.

The essay's title refers to Brodkey's mother's sewing skills and her admonition that a garment would "hang" perfectly only when it was cut "on the bias," that is, across the grain of the fabric. Brodkey uses the term to suggest not only work that is done at odds with (and therefore requiring more care and more risk than) traditional rules demand but also work completed from a particular perspective, a perspective wrought of both principle and passion. In this sense, bias harks back to its popular definition, recognizing one's own prejudicial slant on an issue. Brodkey states, "Even more than what I finally produce, that I do not even attempt to write an essay until I have found a bias would please her, for my practice as a writer is as intricately tied to seeking and following oblique lines that cut across the grain as was my mother's" (545). Writing on the bias extends rather than limits perspectives; it recognizes that "there are at least as many biases woven into the fabric of a life as into poplins, wools, and satins" (546). In Burke's terms, it acknowledges that there any number of representative anecdotes we might adopt as our lens of explanation. Moreover, it acknowledges each discursive effort as a construal, exploiting for its own purposes critique or justification, even when these purposes are contradictory.

Brodkey underscores both the various "biases" and the interpretability of the stories she tells about her childhood recollections, emphasizing that her narrative is one of many and, in fact, may not even be "accurate." In one case, describing a family story in which, at the age of four, she took on the role of neighborhood census taker, she undercuts any claims to external truth free of interpretation. Using the subjunctive, she asserts, "I would like to think that the story of my pre-school experience sustained me through what I now remember as many lean years of writing in school." But then she contradicts this construal, stating, "Yet when I look back I see only a young girl intent on getting it right" (528).

Brodkey's essay repeatedly admits that personal experience, memory, and narrative operate subjectively and ideologically, that other narrators would tell alternative versions. At one point, she remembers being sent to the cloakroom, isolated as punishment for talking during a silent reading period. Describing her terror behind the closed door, she notes that such punishment "ignores the conflict that the middle-class practice of reading alone and in silence, only what is assigned when it is assigned, created in a working-class child whose reading had, until then, been part and parcel of the social fabric of home" (536–37). Later, however, Brodkey acknowledges, "I can see differences in how from one bias I construe the cloakroom as an effort to eradicate traces of working-class sociality from a classroom, and from another I could justify the teacher who sent me there, for I am also a teacher" (546). "Writing on the Bias" emphasizes in deliberate ways that experience is never "authentic," that rather, from the start, it is always socially marked and interpreted. Essays such as Brodkey's provide reassurance that we need not, or more accurately, cannot expect that our students' personal accounts will capture their "true" experiences.

Experience as Fiction in Student Writing

Chief among objections to teaching personal forms of writing to first-year students is concern that it fosters in developing writers a naive investment in some kind of "pure" and unmediated disclosure. For this reason, it is important that students and teachers appreciate the ways in which experience is rhetorically assembled. Because our accounts of lived experience are constantly being reoriented and revised, we must recognize that often our memory gaps are filled with "false" memories ("remembered" from photographs, family stories, and so on).

Further, we must understand that nonfiction writers often purposively amplify or augment their narratives to sustain coherence and clarity. Just as they admit to constructing selves in their texts, autobiographers, memoirists, and essayists will "confess" not only their fictive reconstructions of lived events but also their intentionally creative portrayals of themselves as trustworthy narrators, portraying autobiographical "truth" as a process of creation.[5] Mary McCarthy's collection of autobiographical essays, *Memories of a Catholic Girlhood*, is the case most commonly cited to illustrate that as "the reader and the autobiographer gaze into the unfathomability of memory . . . [they must] concede that the telling of lies is inextricable from the writing of memories" (Gillmore 70–71). In the running commentary that accompanies her essays, McCarthy admits to rearranging the events of her life to "make 'a good story' out of them" and to creating certain dialogues and scenes that are "mostly fictional" (qtd. in Eakin, *Fictions* 10–11; Gillmore 120–24). Recent analyses of autobiographies, ranging from Benjamin Franklin's and Mark Twain's to Jean-Paul Sartre's and Jamaica Kincaid's, confirm that the so-called "autobiographical pact,"[6] the author's guarantee of verifiable, referential truth, is (and probably always has been) itself a fiction.[7] (Most nonfiction writers distinguish between constructed experience as defined by postmodern theory and willful fabrication with intent to hoax. I will address this issue in more detail in the next section.)

Viewed from this perspective, accounts of personal experience for academic purposes might be understood in much the same way that contemporary scholars of autobiography view that genre, "as both an art of memory and an art of imagination." Eakin notes that "memory and imagination become so intimately complementary in the autobiographical act that it is usually impossible for autobiographers and their readers to distinguish between them in practice" (*Fictions* 5–6). By these standards, it seems naive to expect from life writers accurate, factual portrayals of their lived experience drawn from memory. Indeed, we might find that many first-year writing students are quite adept at imaginatively rendering their memories.[8]

For example, Mike, a student in my basic writing class, wanted to recount his childhood trauma of believing that he had injured his father and to explore its implications. Mike's first draft was a thin, chronologic narrative: Mike's father, who had a history of serious back problems, delighted in carrying his two young sons piggyback. One eventful day, as they were playing, the father suffered a ruptured disk. His subsequent hospitalization and Mike's feelings of culpability, Mike suggested, produced in Mike a self-doubting and overly solicitous personality. As is typical of many developing writers, Mike's essay was light on detail and, as such, lacked rhetorical force, yet Mike insisted that he had written "all that [he] could remember" about the occasion.

Since the "facts" surrounding the event were limited by Mike's memory, the essay was doomed to be short and underdeveloped. To continue writing, Mike had to give himself permission to imagine as well as to record his memories. Therefore I suggested that he redraft the narrative in the voice of the child he once was; at the same time, I kept pressing him to sustain enough of his own young adult voice to project his current distance from the event. By casting his essay as a double-voiced narrative—a story within a story—he began to see a sharper division between the two "characters" (the child and adult Mikes), each with their own dramatic purposes. Mike began to fill in the details, perhaps from fresher moments of recall or perhaps from creatively imagining back in time. His final draft includes this paragraph, which did not appear in the original and may or may not be wholly invented:

> As a six-year-old, I thought that I had broken my daddy's back. So after my mom took my father to the hospital, I ran up into my bedroom, sat down in the back of my closet on top of all my brother's and my shoes, and cried for almost twenty-four hours out of guilt for what I thought I had done. Every now and again I would cuddle my head against my grandmother's silk fur coat, which we kept in the closet. I kept repeating aloud to anyone in my house and anyone in heaven who could hear me, "I want my daddy." Now I thought to my fragile self, "I did not just break my daddy's back, I must have killed him, all because I wanted a horsy back ride. How could I be so selfish?" After three months of recovery, my father was back on his feet, but Kevin and I didn't even ask for rides anymore.

In truth, I do not believe there really was a grandmother's silk fur coat, and there may not have been a closet. In the course of writing, however, Mike learned to fill in the gaps with language that creates reality even as it tries to recapture it. Such effort on the part of students recognizes the fictivity of all writing. Reconstructing experience enables students to try on the voices they hear around them, to get in touch with their own perceptions through the freedom of distance, and to use writing to experiment with different narrative viewpoints. (I discuss this point in greater detail as an instructional method in chapter 5.)

In her recent book *Relocating the Personal,* Barbara Kamler insists that foregrounding the fictivity of personal experience writing is an essential attribute of the genre. If adequate and purposive critical work is to be accomplished both through and on the personal, then readers and writers of the personal must acknowledge its textuality and thus its representivity. Kamler chooses the key term *story* in place of *voice* to reinscribe the "separation . . . between the writer's life and the experience she is writing about. What the writer produces is a text, a story, that comes from her but is *not* her" (emphasis in original). As a result, the critic, teacher, or colleague is invited to "ask writerly questions about the personal without critiquing the writer's life" (177). This is what happened when my student Robert wrote an essay about the cultural, social, and economic forces that shaped the development of his personality, using the tone and language we find in these representative paragraphs.

> My advanced maturity arose from the events that shaped my early life. Although my desires were always stifled, the moments that compromised my childhood created a knowledgeable and understanding being.
>
> Money was the main impasse. I had been taught the concept so many years ago, I always believed the knowledge of its purpose was genetic. At five years of age, I knew when the mortgage was due, the first of the month. I knew when tuition payments were to be made, and when the utilities were due. No one ever had to explain to me that I could not have this or that right now. At five, I already felt it best to keep my mouth shut and not ask for a multitude of commercial products that blazed through the television set. I could not even imagine asking for another pair of shoes. I knew the answer would be an embarrassing and shameful "No, not yet!"

When I first read Robert's essay, I thought he was making a misguided attempt to reproduce the inflated language some students characterize as academic discourse, but as I talked with him, I discovered that this was not the case. Robert said that he wanted to recount a true experience, using a narrator who was an older, more sophisticated version of himself. An avid reader, he was trying to replicate the voice of the narrator in works like Joyce's "Araby" or Dickens's *David Copperfield*. Most important, he said that he wanted to make his account "interesting" by creating "an interesting character" to tell it. Obviously, Robert perceived his memoir as a reconstruction. Because he wasn't worried about its authenticity as much as he was concerned about its effect as text, he was deliberately constructing a narrative subject, as described in chapter 2, as well as a narrative experience for this subject to disclose.

Kamler asks readers (and writers) of the personal to examine how an event is "portrayed, which aspects are included, excluded, emphasized, metaphored and with what effects" (177). Robert's story includes the following verifiable "facts": his parents were Colombian citizens; his mother had immigrated to the United States, but his father had been unable to obtain an exit visa and so remained in Columbia; he lived his early life with a grandmother in Spain but traveled widely in both Americas; he loved to read. He describes economic hardship on the part of the family and constructs scenes that recognize conflict and desire.

> I then had a wardrobe that consisted of a private school uniform, a dress suit, matching shoes, a rag tag, faded, blue overall outfit, and a pair of sneakers. There was a sense of taboo woven into my play clothes. If I ruined them, as I was inclined to do at age five, I knew there would not be another playtime outfit soon to follow.

When I worked with Robert, we were able to acknowledge the narrativity of his experience. We could recognize that the fictive narrator's *work* did more than retell the writer's actual experience, that it quite deliberately constructed particular class and

cultural assumptions about children in Western culture outside the
United States. In discussions of personal experience, Kamler writes, "the construct of narrative . . . allows the teacher to foreground the craft of
writing as social and textual construction, a deliberate making."
Robert had already figured this out. He was already using the text
"to create greater agency" and to "reposition [himself] as a text-
worker" (178). As a result, I could help him develop his essay by
asking questions about his fictive narrator rather than focusing on
his actual experiences: What did the narrator think as he recounted
his childhood in Spain and in America? What was the narrator
implying about the loneliness of childhood and the man he had
become? Because the narrator was not Robert, or perhaps a different version of Robert, we worked on the writer's stylistic project of
fulfilling the narrator's purposes.[9]

Kamler makes it clear that efforts to expose the textuality of personal experience are finally intended to "treat stories as a learned
cultural practice," able to be analyzed in relation to cultural contexts
of production, "rather than just celebrated or surveilled for the right/
wrong voice" (46). As I reconsider my engagement with Robert, I
realize that we did not do enough of this analytical work; we were
content to let his text stand for itself, without naming or defining
the critical questions about class and culture that motivated his narrative choices. Kamler suggests that teachers of the personal need to
be more keenly aware of the cultural critical potential of the personal
so that the experience-based writing inscribes not only relocation but
also reflectivity. Through telling stories and reflecting on how we
might reconfigure those tales, we learn to view our lives through alternate lenses of possibility. It is through this reflection that the writer
engages in ongoing transformations of his or her subjectivity.

For Robert, the personal narrative was an effective way to accomplish his goals as a writer. However, Robert's understanding of
both his experiences and his text would have been modified also by
advancing his essay toward personal academic discourse. Working
with Michelle on "Nature's Lessons," I encouraged her to use her
experiences to reconsider the arguments of her source texts. In

Robert's case, I might have taken the opposite approach. Indeed, I might have introduced Robert to relevant scholarly arguments and invited him to engage in cultural critique, to blend his insights with published social or philosophical texts, and to formulate his own theories. (In chapter 4, I use a published personal narrative to explain how such changes might be accomplished.)

As Mike's and Robert's essays reveal, even without our guidance, students may take it upon themselves to exploit the fictive potentiality of personal writing in order to experience a new location and, hence, a different way of seeing the world. Mike found a strategy for adding depth and detail to his experience and, from that vantage point, to interrogate his childish self-blame. Robert figured out a way to manipulate his narrative voices as he worked to create *literary* nonfiction.

Kamler suggests that teachers and therefore students need to develop "a greater self-consciousness about how narratives are told, how they are made, how they might be written differently, how they support, undermine and struggle with other stories, how their writing affects both the teller and the told" (46). She shows how students can recover the rhetoricity of experience by reading personal writing, both their peers' and their own, exclusively *as text*. Offering a deconstructive approach, her students probe for what is hidden, unsaid, or offered too lightly in the essay's language and thus what is "given away" about its social sites, values, and assumptions. In such analysis, questions of truth, authenticity, and accuracy are put aside; the reader's work involves textual analysis, which places the experience into a political context and offers an opportunity to theorize its construction.

The Obligations of Experience as Representation

Yet the matter is complicated. Finding his work described as fictive in an academic journal, essayist Scott Russell Sanders asserts his "shock" and "outrage" while conceding that on a number of levels, he had creatively "shaped" his narrative (40). To explain his reaction, Sanders invokes the notion of the writer's stance toward his or her material: an effort to "preserve and record and help give voice to a reality that existed independently of [the writer]." Refusing to claim "external truth" as his referent, Sanders chooses instead to recognize that "the raw matter of experience, torn away from the axes of time and space, falls in constantly from all sides, undergoes the mind's inscrutable alchemy, and reemerges in the quirky, unprecedented shape of an essay" (41). Sanders's metaphysics emphasizes that despite their willingness to acknowledge their literary reconstructions and imaginative renderings, writers of experience-based prose generally want to stop short of labeling their work fiction.[10]

It does seem to be the case that readers who fully appreciate the limits of truthfulness and accuracy still read nonfiction "differently," expecting at least some correlation between the writer's experience (or memory of that experience) and the events described. Thus Bronwyn T. Williams describes himself as feeling "duped" and "betrayed" in learning that Binjamin Wilkomirski's *Fragments* was fabricated. The exposed inauthenticity of this autobiographical account of childhood survival in German concentration camps gives Williams the sense that "the real stories of children who had suffered had been somehow damaged by his [Wilkomirski's] duplicity" (296). Clarifying the conditions of the autobiographical pact, Sidonie Smith and Julia Watson explain that "while [readers] understand that the source text—the memories of the author—is not accessible or verifiable in any literal sense, [they] are unwilling to accept intentional duping," and they characterize an autobiographical hoax as "potent and politically charged" (32).

But as a journalist, creative writer, and composition instructor, Williams underscores the ambiguities in experiential accounting. In "Never Let the Truth Stand in the Way of a Good Story," he presents an analysis in "three voices" that explore from different angles truth and lying in both the moral and extramoral sense. Williams's title refers to his father's penchant for autobiographical embellishment at the same time that he insisted on his son's unconditional honesty. According to Williams, the effect of this mixed message was his own passionate interest in journalism, a compulsion for recording factual details, even as he honed his skills as an excellent fabricator and ultimately as a writer. Now, as a teacher, Williams must confront these multiple perspectives when he explains to undergraduate writers about current notions of truthfulness, radical undecidability, and memory, and urges them to question complacent self-certainties. Reporting that his students exhibit a range of responses, from complete resistance to cynicism to postmodern impatience, Williams asserts that all of these reactions are "too easy, [and] too definitive" (298–99). He admits that when he reads experience-based nonfiction, he finds himself unwilling to read the text's "truths" as constructs and potently asks, "If I had to question every fact and observation I encountered, what would be the point of reading nonfiction?" (300).

Williams seems to reconcile these competing tensions by presenting them as complementary pedagogical goals.

> I want my students to understand that "truth" is elusive, constructed, and that writing nonfiction can blur the already fuzzy lines between truth and a good story. At the same time I want them to have a deep respect for the best honesty they can muster and, most of all, to have a deep and constant consideration for the consequences of their writing on the people represented by their words. (301)

However, he doesn't stop there, for his essay offers two competing conclusions. In the first, which begins "My father always said, 'Never let the truth stand in the way of a good story,'" he admits that "as an essayist I am prone to stretch the truth as far as I can [while a]s a journalist I worry over the social construction of truth and what parts of stories never get told" (302). These satisfying contradictions are (re)placed in the final "Coda," which begins "My father never said, 'Never let the truth stand in the way of a good story'" (303) and which deconstructs the dashing, creative parent in favor of a more "honest" and more distressing version.

Although as reader, I like the first father better, want to identify with and believe in him, Williams's closing section unsettles the discussion, keeping the fiction and truthfulness of experience in suspension. Because of its uncertainties, because as Lynn Bloom states in her equally important essay addressing this question, "There is no question about whose truth gets told in creative non-fiction—it has to be the author's, with all other truths filtered through the authorial rendering" ("Living" 286), Williams's discussion is one I want to share with my students as I talk about their obligations as nonfiction writers. At the same time, I want to help them to develop a more sophisticated understanding of experiential reconstruction and representation.

The "Truth" about Contexts

From the standpoint of academic evidence, we must also bear in mind that the contexts from which experiential writing emerges are, in and of themselves, significant. As Douglas Hesse warns, we must take care not "to trivialize the importance of knowing whether something is factual or fictional nor to dismiss the effect on a reader of that information." He points out that "the survivors of the Holocaust have crucial reasons for fighting to preserve its events as real and not to allow them to lapse into legend or . . . lie" ("Boundary Zone" 100; similar point in Himmelfarb 144–54), as was the case with Wilkomirski's book. Feminists make a similar point: ignoring or neutralizing the history, the context, and the precise circumstances in which particular women have lived, worked, and written risks misreading that history and misinterpreting those texts.

However, readings that grant the "reality" of experience are likewise fraught with challenges. Especially for members of marginalized groups, invoking one's experience as an agent, witness, or survivor to be the ground of evidence often colludes with those who would construct the marginalized category, "tak[ing] as self-evident the identities of those whose experience is being documented and thus naturaliz[ing] their difference" (Scott, "Evidence" 777). Thus, although feminist historians have questioned claims to the possibility of objectivity and have displaced traditional historical narratives with alternative readings that account for women's experience,[11] recent scholarship warns that this approach may fail to interrogate the construction of female subjectivity as a category or fail to examine the impact on identity formation of agency, race, sexuality, politics, domination, and so on (Scott, "Evidence" 787). Feminists in many disciplines are calling attention to this complexity by reflecting on the political and practical limits of using personal experience in academic writing. They note how difficult it is to reconcile the force of texts that testify as witness or survivor stories when autobiography is understood as socially constructed (Dubrow 14). They observe that personal testimony may become a "trap" if experience-based writers feel themselves attacked when their evidence is interrogated or debated (Scott, "Rejoinder" 400). Rather than attempting to resolve these concerns, Scott emphasizes their irreconcilability. She urges researchers to historicize and contextualize identities produced by claims to experience and to interrogate the language used to represent experience and its role in the process of subject formation. "Experience in this definition," Scott says, "then becomes not the origin of our explanation, not the authoritative (because seen or felt) evidence that grounds what is known, but rather that which we seek to explain, that about which knowledge is produced" ("Experience" 26). Recognizing identity formation as a discursive event, recognizing that experience is construed by and through language and hence entails multiple meanings and interpretations, Scott says, "open[s] new possibilities for analyzing discursive productions of social and political reality as complex, contradictory processes" ("Evidence" 793–94).

Constructing Experience in Composition Research

In composition studies, scholars who use personal writing try to emphasize the complexities and contradictions implicit in experiential evidence, to recognize as Scott does that experience is not something that we *have;* rather it is what conditions who we are. (Scott quotes Teresa de Lauretis: "Experience is the process by which, for all social beings, subjectivity is constructed" ["Experience" 27].) Many, like Gesa E. Kirsch and Joy S. Ritchie, stress the effects of history, society, culture, and biology on our values and beliefs, on the way we perceive and thus frame our experiences. As researchers, the preconstituted lenses by which we view the world obviate claims to objectivity and require critical consideration of our "locations" and subjective positions (11).

A "politics of location" is evident in Karen Surman Paley's *I-Writing*, which presents a method for blending personal and academic writing that openly works to reconcile issues of subjectivity, the social construction of experience, and writer and subject representation. In this ethnographic study, Paley examines two expressivist writing classes for their instructional sophistication and their political and social awareness. Writing in the first person, Paley combines academic research and personal response to insist that her account is simply a reading, positioned, biased, and socially constructed. Further, she states candidly, "[I]n writing up my observations, I found there was no way to mask my opinions. There is neither a neutral posture nor neutral language" (x).[12]

By marking her own ethnicity, academic status, political activism and affiliations, Paley reveals her location politically, socially, and in the context of the material she is observing. In this manner, she foregrounds her obligation as a feminist researcher to "explicitly acknowledge" her "political commitments in relation to the research" (Addison and McGee 3) and to self-consciously claim their subjectivity. Therefore she discloses her experiences with antiwar activism in the 1960s, her Jewish ethnic roots, and her mother's alcoholism, which becomes significant to her analysis of a student writer whose father was alcoholic. Moreover, she openly praises and criticizes her research subjects, both teachers and students, explaining her emotional reactions to their various behaviors and speculating about how she might have handled similar circumstances. Describing a writing conference between an expressivist writing instructor, Helena, and her student, Janet, whose essays and classroom pronouncements about homeless people reflected self-righteousness and middle-class stereotyping, Paley asserts, "I was often frustrated both by the way that Janet presented herself as an expert on the subject of the homeless and by the way that her teacher allowed her to maintain that subject position" (58). Further, she takes care to analyze her emotional responses in relation to her history and experience. As such, she understands that her frustration with Janet is a form of identification: remembering her own political naïveté early in the Vietnam War, she states, "My insight was that I had been impatient with Janet because she reminded me of a self I would just as soon forget" (58).

Repeatedly, Paley uses personal writing to locate herself in relation to her ethnographic observations of student writers and their teachers—in Catherine's family's problems, she identifies her own alcoholic mother; in Tanya's unjust treatment, she recognizes her own status as a Jewish person in a predominantly Catholic university; in her impatience with Helena's circumspect demeanor, she measures her own activist inclinations. By boldly revealing her various affiliations and biases, Paley the researcher reminds readers that "the very words the researcher chooses and the situations he or she reports reflect the researcher's own values and subjectivities" (45). Thus Paley confirms that her rendering of these classrooms is only one reading, and that there are many other ways the stories might be told.

To reinforce this insight, Paley incorporates the voices of her subjects into her ethnographic narratives, a gesture that underscores the complexity and possibility of using personal accounts in scholarly research. In addition to direct quotations from interviews, conversations, and e-mail correspondence, square brackets record her respondents' comments about Paley's observations, and their reactions are interwoven directly into the text at relevant junctures. In this way, Helena expresses her objections to Paley's reading of her engagement with Janet, which characterizes the teacher as unwilling to challenge the student's conservative assumptions about poverty and homelessness. Quoting Helena directly, "I don't expend my energy trying to change a mind that refuses to change at that moment" (85), Paley also includes glosses that give us deeper insight into Helena's teaching philosophy as contrasted with Paley's. Helena writes, "Because you didn't see the product you wanted *at the end of our semester* does not mean that (Janet's intellectual growth was not fostered)" (84, emphasis in original). Repeatedly, Paley allows participants to speak for themselves, even as their statements undermine her interpretation of events. If traditional standards of argument are applied, Paley's reflective, multilayered, first-person approach might seem to undermine confidence in the "truth" or validity of her evidence. Yet the opposite occurs: competing narratives overlap and complicate each other; participants' contrary interpretations enrich her account and bolster readers' confidence in the multiple "truths" that might be gleaned. This is Paley's epistemic accomplishment in *I-Writing*. Her approach, simultaneously confessional, retrospective, reflective, expository, scholarly, and argumentative, presents one model for blending personal and academic discourse in the presentation of scholarly research.

A different though equally complex approach to personal academic writing appears in Kathleen Blake Yancey's chapter "On Feminist Research: What Do Women Want (Now)?, or A Query Regarding Con/Textual Relationships," which appears in *Feminist Empirical Research: Emerging Perspectives on Qualitative and Teacher Research.* In her essay, a reflection on four research studies that appear in the same volume, Yancey uses a highly audible first-person narration to remind readers of the interpretive nature of her scholarly observations. The first sentence—"I have to tell you, right here and now, right from the very beginning of this chapter, that I don't presume any special expertise on the topic of feminist research" (145)—sets the tone for the rest of the essay. The narrator is a human being, with biases and conflicts, who makes no claims to specific expertise. From the first clause, *I* and *you* are on equal grounds, engaged in a conversation that hopefully will offer new insights, a point Yancey states directly at the close of the first paragraph, "I think we might learn something here—together" (145), as she invites her readers' participation.

While an appeal to the personal is often an opening gambit in academic writing, in this piece, it is sustained through the entire chapter. Response to each of the research essays is subtitled "How Do I Read '[title of particular essay]'?" emphasizing that Yancey's reading is one of many that are possible, as the first-person narrator analyzes, reflects, and responds. Discussing Margaret Lindgren's

"Beginning Adult Women Students as College Writers," for example, Yancey writes, "That's one thing I learn here, about how students unpack what we say, about how difficult it apparently is to write responses that students will interpret as we'd hoped." Using italics to highlight textually her reader response, she asserts, "*I like the focus on adult women as students, and I like how different they are; we see unity and diversity at once*" (147). Similarly, she records her reaction to the use of the term *feminine* to replace *feminist* in Janet Bean's "Feminine Discourse in the University": "The *first thing I notice, of course, is the slippage in the term.* . . . Does this matter? I think so . . . I still resist this. I read on" (152).

For Yancey, the audible first-person voice of interpretation helps to subvert patriarchal discourse and its reification of patriarchal knowledge structures, which deny the subjectivity of meaning making and the significance of experiential evidence. Yancey actively solicits reader participation in the knowledge-making process by indicating her own conflicts and desires in response to the texts she is reading, by posing questions that relate the texts to her experiences in the classroom, and by choosing first-person plural to stand for "teachers of composition." Often too she converses directly with the reader by means of second-person pronouns and direct address, invoking at one point the nineteenth-century novel's "Dear Reader" to stress the importance of textual form in the construction of meaning (155) and several times using "See" (as in "You see") to emphasize her point while inviting the reader's response.[13] Yancey's narrator is audible in so much of her essay that she can shift to analysis while maintaining an interpretive edge to her writing. In this way she offers a method for negotiating the dilemma she describes as central to all academic writing: "How to generate the insights of an analysis without its dismembering effects" (154).[14]

Texts like Paley's and Yancey's deliberately emphasize that appeals to personal experience are socially and culturally mediated reconstructions of context-bound events, filtered through interpretation and deployed strategically to fulfill rhetorical purposes. Rather than claiming absolute truth, they illustrate various rhetorical strategies that may be used to signify the complexities and contradictions in experiential representations of self and others. They illustrate too that at least in some academic settings, rhetorically constructed experience is already in use as evidence. These essays (and some others) have tested the waters of personal academic writing and found an audience on board. What a welcoming invitation to composition teachers and students to similarly embark.

"Making" Aunt Rosie

This chapter has focused on the constructed nature of the experiences that we live day to day. Using classroom and published essays, I have tried to show that since writers and readers of the personal acknowledge that experience is conjured in memory and constituted in language and is therefore constructed interpretively, critical concerns about its external truth claims are unwarranted. In closing, I want to return to Michelle's essay "Nature's Lessons" and, in particular, the story of Aunt Rosie.

Reflecting on the passion of Dillard's weasel, Michelle writes, "Dillard is explaining how intense this weasel was and how she could never have had the same meeting with a human. Dillard thinks that humans are incapable of such feelings because we do not need to live with such intensity." Then, to emphasize the rarity of such experience, Michelle invokes a family tale about her aunt, who "has experienced such intense feelings that in one moment her life changed forever." She continues with details of this love-at-first-sight encounter.

> She was sitting in a crowded cafe when all of a sudden the tall, dark, and skinny man of her dreams strolled into the crowded cafe and ordered a blueberry muffin. When he turned to find a seat, her eyes met his and locked. All they could focus on was each other.

I will present the complete anecdote and have more to say about Michelle's use of illustrative example in the next chapter. At this point, I want to remark on the process by which Aunt Rosie came into narrative being, for she was not mentioned in Michelle's early drafts. In fact, Michelle introduced the paragraph at my suggestion. In e-mail, I had asked whether she could think of a good example from her own experience or from her family's history that would help readers to better understand about "animal intensity." In her next draft, we had this story.

I really don't know how many details have been filled in through years of family tradition and retelling. Were her uncle's physical features part of the original account? Did some older family member add that detail over the years, or did Michelle draw on old photos to supplement her rendering? Was there actually a blueberry muffin? Certainly, the smoker in the nonsmoking section, described as the story continues, feels a bit anachronistic. For a while, I even suspected that Aunt Rosie was herself a fiction, although the fact that the story doesn't mesh smoothly into the essay's framework convinces me otherwise. (How much more fitting for the dark stranger to have walked away!) In the end, I don't want to ask Michelle whether the cafe encounter really happened or whether her family believes it happened or whether Aunt Rosie and her husband say it happened. In the end, I just don't want to know.

4 / Valuing Personal Evidence

By the time Michelle and I talk again, we both know that something important has happened. It isn't just that "Nature's Lessons" has grown from a two-page comparison of the mind-sets of skunks and weasels to a complex five-page examination of the limits of human nature. It's also that Michelle's draft is now moving in several significant directions. She tries to contain its multiple perspectives, allowing for Dillard's concept of intensity, Erich's notion of emotional constraint, and her family's real and artificial constructions of natural living. There is a new section about azaleas, as well as the tale of Aunt Rosie and the passionate glance. There is a change in the closing section that struggles to encompass the goals of "sitting back to enjoy the moment" with "learning to live in it." It's true that Michelle's draft now looks more like a personal essay than a literary analysis, and in that sense, we will need to talk next about how she might refocus it. However, the strides she has made are worth the trade-off. The shift and turns in Michelle's thinking, which lead finally to multiple understandings that cannot seem to be reconciled, reveal most clearly the value of reading her own experiences into what was initially a brief analytic paper. Later in this chapter, I will label this attributive, or epistemic, effect of combining personal and academic discourses as a *surplus*—a supplementary that adds to and replaces. Even now we can see that as the personal supplements the academic and the academic supplements the personal, Michelle's essay becomes a text through which she reconceives her understanding of the texts that shape her knowledge of the world.

Yet, even as I have described in some detail newer models of composition discourse, I am haunted by the reasons that many composition theorists would provide to object to my teaching Michelle and her classmates to write personal academic arguments. Some of these reasons, those dealing with subject construction, truth and authenticity, and the nature of experience, I've rehearsed in some detail, and I have tried to show how feminist and postmodern theories provide answers to or obviate those concerns. In this chapter, I emphasize the intellectual project that is (or can be) experience-based writing and discuss at length what is gained evidentially and epistemically when we use personal and academic arguments together. Drawing from Aristotle, I will discuss the personal narrative as logical induction or reasoned example. Turning to orientation theories developed by Kenneth Burke, Walter R. Fisher, and James C. Raymond, I will show that personal academic argument can generate richer and more complex surplus meanings than either personal or academic evidence alone. Finally, I will examine questions of validity for personal writing in two published essays and suggest a way to supplement, and therefore to rewrite, experiential evidence.

Personal Reason(s)

We often seem to forget that the classical tradition invites us to use experience as evidence. In the *Rhetoric,* Aristotle advises speakers to take advantage of three means of persuasion in constructing (inventing) arguments for public address: logos, ethos, and pathos. In earlier chapters, I have taken into account personal appeals that enhance the character of the writer or excite the emotions of the audience, and because rhetorical theorists often describe such appeals in terms of voice or narrative persona, it's easy to see why personal writing would work well in these situations. For Aristotle, however, the rhetor's most intellectually rigorous work is demonstrated by his use of logic.[1] It thus remains for us to see how personal narratives—both brief and extended—can make the kinds of logical arguments privileged by Aristotle and by many present-day academics.

Admittedly, Aristotle does not conjure personal experience stories in his *Rhetoric*. However, to support his methods, he draws on a host of examples from the political events and speeches of his day, references bound to be familiar to students of his text. Kate Ronald explains that because, in the fourth century, the political realm and private life were more deeply enmeshed than today, students of rhetoric would have felt immediately and intimately linked to the topics recommended for rhetorical training, such as war and peace or types of governments (Ronald 42). Countering observations that classical rhetoric was entirely public in form and content,[2] Ronald observes that "the classical tradition defined rhetoric as an internal way of knowing and investigating one's culture," that it "emphasized a personal relationship between speaker and audience," and that it required speakers to assume personal responsibility for their discourse and its effects (38). Pointing out that much of Aristotle's *Rhetoric* examines both audiences' and speakers' mental activities, Ronald shows that ancient Greek life concerned itself with the student rhetor's investigation of his own intentions and individual learning. Answering Plato's call for an ideal rhetoric, Aristotle's work "can be read as a method of discovering choices in language, and being responsible to an audience for those choices" (42). In Ronald's view, then, the student of rhetoric understood the political as personal and also understood that rhetorical engagement required a personal investigation of the issues to be debated and a personal relationship with the audience. Sidonie Smith and Julia Watson provide additional support for autobiographical leanings in classical Greece. Drawing on an early-twentieth-century work, Georg Misch's *History of Autobiography in Antiquity,* they note that personal references appear "in funerary inscriptions about feats of battle and in early texts such as funeral orations, familiar letters, and travel narratives" (84–85).

For Aristotle, personal experience significantly contributes to persuasive arguments and to subsequent decision making. In *Nicomachean Ethics,* Aristotle places high value on the role of lived experience in the formation and acquisition of practical wisdom. Experience provides the understanding of and familiarity with particulars that are needed for determining an appropriate course of action (6.7–9). Aristotle also supports the use of stories, including those derived from lived experience, explicitly in his discussion of narration in Book 3 of the *Rhetoric* and implicitly in his attention to example in Book 2. For the epideictic rhetoric of praise or blame, Aristotle recommends brief stories arranged throughout a speech to back up specific features or qualities of the individual being described (3.16.1). For judicial rhetoric, the prosecution calls on background narrative to clarify relevant events and describe the manner in which harm or injustice has occurred. For the defense, narrative offers a means of justifying actions (3.16.4–9). In Aristotle's discussion of deliberative oratory, the narrative portion of the speech is used to explore past events, "in order that by being reminded of those things the audience will take better counsel about what is to come" (3.16.11).[3]

Even more significant, the *Rhetoric's* emphasis on evidence by example further warrants narrative and story-making arguments. As Aristotle explains it, there are two main ways to logically construct a rhetorical argument: you can create enthymemes, which are like syllogisms in formal logic, or you can develop paradigms, generally arguments by example, which are similar to dialectical inductions. The chronologic form of much experience-based writing seems closely related to this second kind of evidence building. In drawing this parallel between narrative and example in the *Rhetoric,* I follow on James C. Raymond's observation that Aristotle's examples always assume a diachronic structure.

> Each one is a story, an event leading to another event, like cause to consequence, not with the inexorable determinism of scientific causality, but in a pattern of probable causality, suggesting that if analogous events were to take place again, analogous consequences would be likely to ensue. (146)[4]

According to the *Rhetoric,* examples drawn from both fiction and real life allow the speaker and audience to reason a general rule from particular cases (1.2.8–9, 1.2.19, 2.25.8).[5] Historical examples, in the form of stories of past events, are particularly suitable for deliberating future courses of action because "future events will be like those of the past" (2.20.8). Underscoring the persuasiveness of personal testimony, Aristotle notes that when examples follow a central point, they act like "witnesses and a witness is everywhere persuasive" (2.20.9).

In Michelle's essay, the story about Aunt Rosie functions as narrative example to explain the nature and importance of passion. Michelle focuses on Dillard's conviction, expressed in "Living Like Weasels," that the weasel lives with intensity, the kind of emotion that she reads as rarely accessible to human beings. Then, using the structure of a fairy-tale romance, Michelle recounts the following anecdote, presented here in its entirety.

> I have an Aunt Rosie who has experienced such intense feelings that in one moment her life changed forever. She tells the story of the first time she laid eyes on my uncle. She was sitting in a crowded cafe when all of a sudden the tall, dark, and skinny man of her dreams strolled into the crowded cafe and ordered a blueberry muffin. When he turned to find a seat, her eyes met his and locked. All they could focus on was each other. She says that it was as if the two of them were talking without words. Just looking in this stranger's eyes seemed to tell her all she needed to know about him. According to my aunt, at that moment nothing in the world mattered to her, not the man that was sitting next to her smoking in the non-smoking section, not even the couple two tables away who had just gotten en-gaged. To be so captivated in one person and not even know him—this is the closest feeling that I could compare with the animal magnetisms that the weasel has. Although there are special situations, usually we humans do not take no-tice of every thing around us like the weasel must. We just let people walk by us and think nothing of it.

Michelle's narrative example, an illustration of human—as opposed to weasel—passion, recites the effects of being willing to live in the moment. It is intended to be an object lesson: if we fail to allow for this kind of passionate attention to our surroundings, the one true lover, the man or woman of our destiny, may simply pass by without our even realizing it.

To understand how the tale of Aunt Rosie works as evidence in Michelle's essay, we can follow Raymond's explanation of narrative proof. Raymond first establishes the close relationship between Aristotle's discussions of example and enthymeme. While their formal features appear quite different, Raymond argues, these two central ways to demonstrate proof in a rhetorical argument rely on the same intellectual operations: generalizations emerging from prior assumptions, which are provided by the audience rather than stated by the rhetor. Like syllogisms in formal logic, enthymemes rely on a pattern of premises leading to a conclusion, although "the major premise in an enthymeme may be implied rather than expressed because the audience is presumed to know it" (142). Raymond explains that "because enthymemes presume upon what an audience already knows or believes, they can express in a condensed or elliptical manner chains of logical connections that would be complex indeed if the assumptions themselves had to be demonstrated" (144).[6] Raymond shows that examples demand a similar degree of intellectual rigor, since an example relies on the audience's assumptions to supply the logical leap needed to interpret a general rule from multiple or extended examples. In other words, the "missing middle term" that is supplied by the audience for the enthymemic reasoning is also supplied in the process of drawing a generalization from the particulars in arguments using examples (147) and, I would add, using narratives in the manner described in the *Rhetoric*.[7]

Michelle's example is personal, based in family mythology, rather than verifiable fact. Yet there is no missing the story's value for her essay's larger argument: it is an age-old tale of found—or lost—opportunity, a lesson with general application. The missing middle term is an invocation: Reader, if you were Aunt Rosie, might you have looked away? Been distracted by surrounding smokers and romantic couples? Missed the moment? Have there been, already, opportunities you did not follow? The missing middle term in Michelle's example, the leap from the specific case of Aunt Rosie to the argument in "Living like Weasels" comes by way of (what for many young women seems) a commonplace: Those special few who dare not to look away, who refuse to succumb to life's petty distractions, may discover the momentous gaze of the stranger.

Epistemic Reason(s)

For Aristotle, example is not only evidence provided by way of illustration, as described in Book 2, but also a way of reasoning, as described in Book 1. This second sense of rhetorical example relates to contemporary theorists' notions of narrative thinking. Simply put, it suggests that one way we attempt to understand the world is by organizing it into various stories or plot lines, some of which will serve brief and immediate purposes while others become the basis of cherished beliefs. Because, in narrative, principal components are arranged in time, narrative thinking involves a kind of reasoning different from deductive logic, although it too involves relationships, causal conditions, and so on. When we invoke our experiences as evidence, not only are we asking readers to understand our argument by means of different intellectual processes but also we are operating from a different set of perspectives.

Defining narrative perspective as both "the spatiotemporal coordinates of an agent or observer [within a text, and] . . . the norms, attitudes, and values held by such an agent or observer" (5), Willie van Peer and Seymour Chatman hold that "experience with different narrative perspectives, fictional as well as nonfictional, allows us to view the world from different locations, angles, and value systems" (12). In Kenneth Burke's terms, a concept can be viewed from either a poetic orientation or a rational orientation; in Walter R. Fisher's terms, the writer or reader may employ narrative logic or traditional logic.

Kenneth Burke's notion of orientation helps to explain how perspectives shift and change when we use different methods of reasoning. Burke uses this term to describe "a sense of relationships, developed by the contingencies of experience," including the social, institutional, and economic conditions that shape expectations, desires, values, and decisions. An orientation is both sustained in and perceived by way of our language structures and terminologies (*Permanence* 18). For Burke, there are manifold orientations, although the scientific orientation is the dominant principle of order for our times. Burke says, "Shifts of interpretation result from the different ways in which we group events. . . . Such shifts of interpretation make for totally different pictures of reality, since they focus the attention upon different orders of relationship" (*Permanence* 36). However, because it is so difficult to see beyond our current orientations, Burke encourages us to attempt a "perspective by incongruity," essentially turning our worldview upside down both verbally and conceptually by "re-seeing" it through opposing and paradoxical verbal lenses (*Permanence* 69–124). Thus, to remedy the existing scientific orientation with its inherent instrumentalist, hierarchical, and capitalist values, Burke suggests a poetic orientation, a humanistic, or poetic, rationalization "situated in a philosophy, or psychology, of poetry" (*Permanence* 65–6).[8]

Similarly, in Walter R. Fisher's distinction between the narrative paradigm and the rational world paradigm—the two principal forms by which "humans recount or account for human choice and action" ("Narration, Knowledge" 170)—we find not only competing efforts to communicate but also competing ways to understand the world around us. The dominant notion of knowledge, according to Fisher, is the rational world paradigm of traditional argument. The legacy of positivism, this paradigm privileges objectivity, orchestrating rational arguments based on "self evident propositions, demonstrations, and proofs" ("Narration as" 268). Fisher asserts that deductive rational argument is not our natural orientation; rather human understanding is intrinsically conditioned by narrative insight.[9] Ordinary people generally use narrative reasoning when they investigate real-world issues or determine appropriate courses of actions. Moreover, personal and experiential stories are significant within the narrative paradigm. "The narrative perspective," he observes, ". . . has relevance to real as well as fictive worlds, to stories of living and to stories of the imagination" ("Narration as" 266). In the model Fisher proposes, narrative is broader in its scope than other paradigms, embracing many ways of telling, including the scientific. Hence, objective claims merely disguise their subjective, personal stories ("Narration as" 268–70; "Clarifying" 56). Because narrativity is a dominant form of rationality, Fisher says, all "human communication should be viewed as historical as well as situational, as stories competing with other stories constituted by good reasons" ("Narration as" 266).

When narrative and rational orientations occur within a single text, their competing logics force reorientations: experiential accounts allow us to form new theories; new theories lead to new ways of viewing our experiences; and each approach infuses the other with new questions and alternative answers. Put another way, when we use personal experience as evidence in scholarly writing, we simultaneously frame our subject narratively and deductively, and thus offer our readers (at least) two kinds of understanding or conceptualization.

Michelle's evolving draft reflects this reorientation in her viewpoint as she considers the differences between her admonitions that we should "learn how to enjoy our lives and live in the moment, just as the skunk and weasel do" and the apparently satisfying realities of her family's suburban context. Prompted by our conference conversation, she now suggests that Dillard's ventures in Hollins Pond are, like her own, "a facade," an attempt to make nature out of what is at hand. In subsequent e-mails, I encourage Michelle to push at this point, which seems to me to run counter to her final argument that we must "take the time to listen to nature and understand all it has to offer." I want Michelle to reread Dillard and Erdrich through her newfound appreciation for the concept of "what works for us," a notion gleaned by tapping and then reconstructing her personal experience as evidence. In her draft, I see traces of her earlier position, most evident in her introductory and concluding paragraphs.

At this point, Michelle's developing writing skills compete with the urgency of her newfound insights, and her draft seems unable to contain them both. Through my questions, I try to guide her to construct a richer and more sophisticated analysis of both the published essays and her experience, one that offers less advice, more explicit conflict. My goals are pedagogic and are directed toward Michelle's development as a thinker, an observer, and a writer. Despite the fact that, ultimately, Michelle is unable to finesse the competing claims of her emerging essay, I see that through this braiding of personal and scholarly evidence, she has already arrived at insights that stretch the limits of either an exclusively narrative or an exclusively critical essay.

Fusing Orientations, Constituting Surplus

Fisher asserts that we are always using the narrative paradigm, that it is our most familiar orientation, and that the rational orientation is an artificially conceived subset within it. However, to stress what both Burke and Fisher believe, that narrative and argumentative orientations give us different ways of seeing the same thing, I want to keep these categories separated. Rather than creating a hierarchy of viewpoint values or subsuming one approach into the other, I want to stress the gains of subjecting the same issue to several kinds of understanding. I want to suggest that in some measure, when Michelle combined narrative and academic orientations, she found *surplus,* or insights that she could not fully reconcile because they emerged from different ways of knowing (even though she didn't realize that she was invoking different ways of knowing), and thus she began to resee her issues, attempting to rewrite her essay to reflect their greater complexity.

This notion of *surplus,* as it is used by feminists like Joy Ritchie and Kathleen Boardman, Lynn Worsham, and Joan W. Scott, helps to explain how the fusing of orientations promotes, for writers and readers, a more complicated process of meaning making. Discussing the competing stories that arise from different subjectivities, social frameworks, and viewpoints, they point to the places where meanings and understandings overlap as well as where they diverge. Readers' and writers' competing perspectives add to existing perspectives, creating excesses, enabling us to imagine what was heretofore unimaginable. Describing the emergence of subjectivity as a "discursive event," Scott notes that "there are conflicts among discursive systems, contradictions within any one of them, multiple meanings possible for the concepts they deploy" ("Evidence" 793). As Ritchie and Boardman compare origin stories for various feminist theories, they note a similar effect. In competing narratives, they find "'diverse discourses,' which are in excess of what a singular linear argument requires" (603). Multiple, contradictory interpretations and viewpoints introduce points of disruptive "excess not easily retrofitted as the norm" (Clark, "Argument" 98; qtd. in Ritchie and Boardman 602). Such writing inaugurates a dialectic of overlapping meanings, which Ritchie and Boardman characterize as "inclusion with a difference: uncontained and without limits" (603). At these sites of textual overlap, the *surplus* or supplementarity of opposing narratives of personal experience offer potentially new and more complex meanings.

In other words, such points of excess are epistemic sites: places where our knowledge is re-viewed and reconstituted to account for (but not necessarily to integrate) inherent contradictions. Excess or surplus has greater explanatory power if we view it as a cognate to Jacques Derrida's *supplement,* a term he uses to explain a symbolic action that "adds itself, it is a surplus, a plenitude enriching another plenitude. . . . But the supplement supplements. It adds only to replace" (144–45). In other words, a supplement is both an addition and a substitute—one thing cannot stand in for the other but will simultaneously add to and detract from what the other was thought to be. What emerges by way of the supplement appears as something else entirely. In Derrida's thinking, the supplement is "dangerous" because it challenges traditional ways of thinking and knowing. For my purposes, in thinking personal evidence as the supplement for academic writing, the dual efficacy of experiential and traditional argumentative claims promotes an alternative orientation and a more complicated description of the world.

In a related context, Geoffrey Galt Harpham explains how surplus emerges dialectically when narrative and theoretical conceptual frameworks are juxtaposed in criticism: literature or the literary narrative does not just exemplify (or fail to exemplify) theory; it *excites* it. . . . Narrative engages with theory in a process of reciprocal probing and stressing that tests the capacity of theory to comprehend and regulate practice, and the power of "actual life" . . . to elude or deform theory. (402, emphasis added)[10]

The relationship between personal experience stories and the claims of an academic argument operate in much the same way. Together, the personal and academic effect the "mutual stimulation of theory and example" (402), inaugurating two dialectical processes: one between academic and personal modes and the other among personal modes. Moreover, neither narrative nor deductive argument is supplemental in the usual sense of that word; rather their meanings infuse each other. What results is a *surplus* of meanings, offering us a deeper and more complex appreciation of the issues at stake.

Lynn Z. Bloom's "Living to Tell the Tale: The Complicated Ethics of Creative Nonfiction" weaves just such an effect. The essay, which explores truth telling in experience-based nonfiction, begins with an apparently unrelated scene: Bloom, a graduate student, is being treated in a university hospital emergency room; during the admission process, she confirms an unspoken family secret, that she was born a twin. In the next section, Bloom employs conventional academic discourse, defining terms, citing sources, and explaining varied positions regarding the ethics of autobiographical disclosure. Throughout her essay, Bloom alternates between these modes of presentation, creating layers of meaning that require her audience to read simultaneously by way of personal narrative and deductive orientations. (Bloom's essay illustrates one model of how this cognitive challenge might be realized; to be sure, there are myriad patterns for blending genres.)

Through *story*, Bloom tells how her parents altered her birth records, never spoke about the birth loss of her twin, rejected her for marrying a Jewish man. With meticulous detail, she recreates her father, a scientist and academic, a teller of stories that delight his children, a perfectionist and morose alcoholic. Saturated with ambivalence and longing, the story is told through the eyes of the narrator, who shows the effects of too many secrets. In the alternating sections, Bloom invokes *exposition* and *analysis* to develop a series of carefully researched and firmly supported claims regarding the nonfiction writer's imperative to tell "both the literal and the larger Truth" (278); the selective and interpretive nature of that truth; and the author's crucial shaping of character, point of view, tone, voice, and selection of details (285–86).

I have reread "The Complicated Ethics of Creative Nonfiction" many times over. Each time I am sure that I have determined Bloom's argument, and each time I am inclined to describe it differently. If I read only the narrative, I arrive at one set of convictions: lies and omissions take their toll; autobiography is a birthright. If I read only the academic portions, I discern another: the truths one tells are problematic, changed over time, value-laden, and aesthetically, as well as ethically, driven. When I put these claims together, I see something else entirely: the warp of family secrets about birth records, twinhood, and anti-Semitism and the woof of ethical and aesthetic considerations for writing creative nonfiction are woven tightly together, the supplement supplements, each meaning dependent on the other. As I shift between these narrative and academic orientations, my thinking is challenged at every turn, and I cannot state Bloom's thesis outright. That is what I mean by *surplus*.

The Question of Evaluation

I have been arguing in this chapter that personal experience belongs in academic writing because, first of all, it contributes to the construction of logical arguments much the same as any other illustrative example and, further, because the experiential supplements the propositional to create a surplus, a new kind of understanding that belongs to neither narrative thinking nor analytic thinking alone. Of course, neither of these reasons reconciles the problem of validating experiential evidence, which is a major source of controversy even among advocates of personal and narrative forms.

Before taking up this issue, I want to recognize that for many contemporary scholars, concerns about validity should not apply to methods intended to subvert traditional ideologies and attendant practices. For Kathleen Yancey, invoking *validation*, a term defined by means of positivist paradigms, undermines the goals of feminist rhetoric and aligns the researcher with traditional standards of evidence that function oppressively (155; Brodkey, "Writing Ethnographic" 46–47). Likewise, Wendy Bishop argues that composition research must include student voices and that in doing so, it must challenge positivist research paradigms. She states,

> Reliability is not at issue here; writers as humans are as complex as the communities they form and can never be studied the same way twice, exactly. Validity is not at issue here; we do not always study what we thought we were setting out to study, but we are still learning from reflective practice. ("Students'" 211)

In the view of these writers, traditional paradigms that demand validation procedures devalue narrative and especially underrate personal writing. Nevertheless, for reasons I discuss below, I want to insist that *although we must choose carefully our methods for securing confidence in our evidence, we cannot discount the need to do this particular kind of work.*

In this section, I explain why validity is crucial for securing the status of the personal in academic writing. Using two published personal essays that focus on writing teacher response, I show just how tempting it is to ignore concerns about evidence and to embrace claims backed by personal experience. Borrowing from Raymond and Fisher, I propose some possible ways to interrogate the adequacy of personal evidence. To close this chapter, I return to the notion of surplus to explore what might be gained by supplementing a personal orientation with an academic orientation in one published essay.

When a student writes a paper about an oppressive relationship (Kamler) or confesses to a crime (R. Miller) or admits to drug addiction or some other kind of victimization, we may feel ourselves placed in the awkward position of evaluating a life rather than a text. In fact, even if we construct assignments that discourage disclosure, students will, at times, write confessionally (Morgan). In these cases, of course, we must decide whether we will respond to the issue or problem described in the pages of the text, help the student to improve the text at hand, or recommend a different rhetorical approach to the topic. In other instances, however, when the writing is not discomfiting but rather appropriate to the arguments at hand, we are still left with the dilemma of validation. If the writer says something happened in a particular way from his or her particular perspective, we cannot say that this account is inaccurate or that the writer needs to reconceive the experience from a different vantage point (although we may try at times to do just that). Richard Flores eloquently captures a central problem for experiential evidence.

> The personal seemingly stifles this process [of validation] by silencing the judgments and critiques of others. How are my evaluative peers to assess my scholarly work that is fastened to my experience of growing up in south Texas beneath the watchful eye of those whose views of Chicanos were blatantly racist? Could my peers write in their reviews that my account is incorrect and that I must reconsider my experience? How do they argue with my lived reality? We can dismiss the theoretical arguments of others as immaterial to a particular case, but it is more difficult to claim that lived experience, when used to verify a scholarly position, is invalid or irrelevant. (1166)

If personal experience cannot be nullified or negotiated, how can we determine which stories should count as evidence, which stories are appropriate to the case at hand?[11]

Moreover, as Heather Dubrow observes, "Turning an object into evidence is like gift-wrapping it: the agent performing the action defines and delimits the significance of the object" (16). Because evidence is constructed rhetorically and then accepted and endorsed as material by readers as much as by writers, no fact or story is of itself evidence. As a result, there is an intimate relationship between evidence and power: what counts as evidential is determined by those positioned to credential and validate particular objects or discourses while discounting alternative interpretations (Dubrow 16).[12] Writing teachers who evaluate their students' personal accounts have likely felt the authority implicit in endorsing a writer's experience as evidential.

Clearly, the methodological limit of the experiential account is the supreme achievement of the personal as well as its greatest shortcoming. Personal writing is highly seductive because it invites readers to "simply" identify even as it moves them toward acquiescence. Consequently, if we don't find a way to submit personal evidence to rigorous examination, we surrender to critics who discount it as merely subjective and therefore inadequate for academic purposes. To emphasize the need for validation processes, I present two published essays that illustrate just how appealing uninterrogated personal evidence can be.

The narrative "Daisies" was written by Ellen A. Laird, a full-time English instructor at Hudson Valley Community College in Troy, New York, and published recently in *TETYC*. Rummaging through her attic one day, Laird finds a short story, now twenty-nine years old, written by her husband when he was a high school sophomore. At the top of the first page, a grade of ninety-five is boldly circled. No comments or criticism mark the paper, and as she reads, Laird speculates about the kinds of response that she, a conscientious, theory-minded composition instructor, would have offered to this novice writer. Sitting in her attic, Laird reminds herself that her husband, now a successful attorney, exudes justifiable confidence in his writing and language skills. Perhaps, she thinks, Mr. Lewis, her husband's teacher, was on to something. Perhaps comments, criticism, and revised drafts squelch the "vulnerable inner center" of youthful creativity (124). The implied point of the story is that the discipline of composition studies may be misguided in its efforts to foster revision by providing comprehensive responses to student papers. Perhaps it's product, not process, after all.

In contrast is Raymond Carver's essay "Creative Writing 101."

It too is a personal narrative. It too tells about a writing teacher, this time Carver's first creative writing class in his first semester at college, taught by John Gardner, then a struggling novelist. Carver explains the course requirements, a ten- to fifteen-page short story, revised at least ten times during the semester, and he describes his teacher's method of instruction:

> It was a basic tenet of his that a writer found what he wanted to say in the ongoing process of seeing what he'd said. And this seeing, or seeing more clearly, came about through revision. He *believed* in revision, endless revision; it was something very close to his heart and something he felt was vital for writers, at whatever stage of their development. (1584–85, emphasis in original)

Because someone was reading his stories carefully, responding to them, and taking them seriously, Carver says, he developed the confidence and the skills that propelled his career as a noted writer of short fiction. For Carver, then, intervention and process are requisite.

We have here two competing stories, each providing personal experience as evidence. Which do we accept, and what are the consequences of that acceptance? I am captivated by Laird's essay, especially its final paragraphs, which speculate on Mr. Lewis's background, teaching philosophy, and work habits. She writes with humor, "I'd bet my bookbag that he avoided national conferences, let his journal subscriptions lapse, and felt no pressure from within or without the discipline" (124). Despite his inflating her husband's grade, despite his failure to offer comments, inadvertently or instinctively, Mr. Lewis taught "one boy a lesson for a lifetime—that the kid knew how to write." Laird's closing sentences are particularly gratifying. She writes, "It seems Mr. Lewis said what he set out to say: 'You're good, kid. Keep writing. The small stuff will take care of itself.' In this case, Mr. Lewis had it right." (124). To me, this is a wonderful but also dangerous essay. Overworked and exhausted writing teachers, I speculate, might well read in this narrative "proof" that comments and drafting are suspect, they might read it as permission to ignore twenty-some years of composition research in favor of the quick grade.

On the other hand, because I read in Carver's essay "proof" that the strategies I use in my writing classes are sound, I naturally accept his evidence as reliable and valid. This, of course, is exactly the problem. "It is here," as Flores has shown,

> that suspicion must enter. If we accept the notion that scholarship in the humanities is judged not on verifiability but on rhetorically rendered and persuasively fashioned argumentation, we must also be suspicious of attempts to anchor positions in personal experience without discussion. (1166)

Thus, to fight for experiential evidence, we will need to devise a better way to determine judgment.

Fidelity and Probability in Personal Evidence

One way to evaluate evidence is to interrogate the assumptions that readers must accept in order to find an argument valid. James C. Raymond bases his approach on his understanding of the methods required of Aristotle's rhetor and audience as they interactively produced the generalizations necessary for arguments by example or enthymeme. According to Raymond, the critic must thus identify and interrogate assumptions, "both explicit and implicit, that the presumed reader of the text is expected to share, and to locate the paradigms, if any, that form the basis of the argument" (150). To analyze an argument and its effects, Raymond contends, we must realize that readers accept or reject arguments on the basis of mutual assumptions and shared illustrative patterns, not on the strength of proof or evidence per se (150). In the case of personal experience stories, we would examine common assumptions implicit in the move from the writer's specific case to a generalization and then to the reader's analogous construction of this principle within his or her own specific experience.

Similarly influenced by Aristotelian philosophy and rhetoric, but concerned primarily with questions of value in moral choice, Walter R. Fisher's methods of interrogating the narrative paradigm nicely extend Raymond's approach to include all diachronic discourses. Fisher depends on what he terms "a logic of good reasons," a system of rhetorical analysis, based on Aristotle's concept of practical reason, that provides for an evaluation of the values and assumptions embedded in argumentative discourse. Fisher asserts that because stories are an inherent way of organizing and understanding experience, humans instinctively know how to produce and judge stories. All narratives may be evaluated and critiqued for their validity or rationality by applying principles of "*narrative probability,* what constitutes a coherent story," and more significant for my purposes, "*narrative fidelity,* whether the stories they [audiences] experience ring true with the stories they know to be true in their lives" ("Narration as" 272, emphasis in original).

Narrative probability involves the formal features of the story, such as the consistency of characters and actions. In contrast, narrative fidelity is focused on substance; it poses questions about the narrative's relationship to the audience's values and commonplaces as individuals and as members of society. A text or argument that embodies narrative fidelity will, from Fisher's point of view, exhibit ethical and effective rhetorical performance, and this determination will come from asking critical questions about the implicit and explicit values expressed in the message: their implications, their appropriateness, their potential effects on individuals and community; their consonance with the reader's or critic's experience, the experience of others, or the experience implied in the narrative's audience construct; their potential for encouraging human understanding and moral conduct ("Toward" 379–80). Fisher makes it clear that the "logic of good reasons" will not decide the "best" answer among competing sets of "good" values. It will, however, make explicit both the heretofore unarticulated assumptions within the narrative and the values on which those assumptions are based. For Fisher, as for Raymond, judgment of narrative requires an interrogation of the writer's and the audience's assumptions, although in

Fisher's case, the moral efficacy of the assertion will have some bearing on narrative validity.[13]

While it is correct, as critics have argued, that we cannot judge the truth of a writer's sense of his or her own lived experience (we cannot say that an event did not happen in a particular way if the speaker says that it did), we can nevertheless evaluate his or her interpretation of narrative events for its fidelity by examining his or her assumptions.[14] Aristotle shows that an audience will assent to the inductive argument if it recognizes a correspondence between the speaker's illustrations and the generalization that is implied or stated. Both Raymond and Fisher explain that this concordance takes place with the acceptance of shared assumptions. That is, if the narrative is to be deemed reliable, both the writer and the reader must come to the same conclusion regarding the significance of its claims. Putting aside the issue of moral judgment, I want to take from Fisher's method and from Raymond's extensions of Aristotle the interrogation of assumptions as a means of evaluating the arguments in personal experience stories.

Most published articles and much student writing that call upon the personal as evidence will demonstrate narrative probability, that is, plot and character coherence, by virtue of the accessibility of this genre. On some occasions, of course, inconsistencies will be noted and, at times, the absence of sufficient detail may limit the persuasive force of the argument. In the case of Laird's "Daisies," for example, the writer asserts a correlation between her husband's professional success and his high school teacher's rewarding without interference his developing writing skills. She describes a plausible set of actors: the attorney today, the student writer long ago, Mr. Lewis, and the knowledgeable compositionist narrator. Likewise, she charts a clear and logical chronology, engaging a story within a story so that we move from present to past and back again, passing to view a contemporary writing classroom as we travel back to the narrator's attic ruminations. Judging the work's narrative probability, we accept by its adherence to detail that it makes a good story.

Judging the fidelity of the narrative, however, asking whether the claims it makes are consistent with what educators and teachers of writing have experienced or studied, we will accept some of its assumptions and reject others. Most of us will agree that in the writing classroom, criticism can be destructive, that overly critical, overly zealous demands too often result in defensiveness and resistance, and that even the best of writers may need time for readers' comments to settle and soften before they can be assimilated and transformed during revision. But will we accept that the attorney's confidence and professional success result from his tenth-grade English teacher's strategic nonintervention? Might we ask, first, whether the absence of commentary was an intentional act of encouragement by the teacher and, further, whether his student interpreted the response as encouragement? Rather than signaling a kinder, gentler approach to the text, might commentless grading suggest, instead, a lack of interest or respect for the task at hand? Might we also ask whether the student had, subsequently, taken writing courses that contributed to his language skills? Finally, might we question whether particular economic and social pathways enabled him to acquire the confidence he needed to become a successful trial lawyer, who "excelled in a career choice heavily dependent upon highly skilled, especially confident writing and thinking" (124)?

In evaluating this personal narrative, we might also call on current theories about teaching, particularly about writing instruction. Here we find a body of research and a different set of assumptions: that students rarely learn in a vacuum; that only the best readers and the strongest students seem adept in imagining alternative possibilities or moving to the next level of proximal development without guidance; that human beings usually desire acknowledgment of and feedback about the work they do; that most writers seek out readers for direction on revision (because we cannot see our own work as a reader sees it); that students today are learning that writing is not magical and therefore accessible only to those chosen few who already possess the "gift" but rather a process of work and drafts, something that can be taught and therefore learned. In the leap from cause to effect—in the unexplained variables and in the body of educational and composition research that supports formative teacher response—the logic of the argument in "Daisies" breaks down. We cannot accept its implicit assumptions.

In contrast, Carver's narrative is valid not because it supplies more details to help us understand the move from cause to effect (although it does do this in a way that Laird's does not) but because its argument can be judged in light of the same educational research and found consistent with that research to the extent that we are able to confirm it at this historical moment. Moreover, in accepting Carver's assumptions as correlative to our own, we bring to bear an examination of our experiences as students and as teachers receiving and providing reader feedback, including experiences with summative versus formative criticism. And since narratives can be viewed as extended examples from which the reader can extrapolate analogous situations that project into the future, we bring to bear an examination of the patterns of thought and action undergirding each type of response: not only can we ask about the kinds of messages implied in ongoing reader response and whether Carver would have learned painstaking revision without a mentor to guide him, but we can also project into a future of writing instruction focused exclusively on evaluation and anticipate its consequences.

Supplementing the Personal Narrative

Personal writing is problematic not because it's difficult to judge its claims but because the uninterrogated and unevaluated personal narrative is seductive and, consequently, dangerous. Serious research requires that scholars evaluate and test a writer's methods and findings. However, the samples I selected are essays, not typical scholarly articles. While they dramatically illustrate the allure of personal writing, in neither are claims mitigated by research or subjected to the demands of scrupulous justification. It is true that in both essays we sense (but do not hear) the whisper of ongoing academic conversations about the nature of revision, intertextuality, collegial reader response, and various pedagogic theories. But these issues are not inscribed directly in the texts.

In my discussion of Michelle's essay, I tried to show how the supplement of personal experience changed Michelle's vantage point and gave her a new and broader way to conceive her argument. Now I want to ask the opposite question: What would happen if theory were blended into Laird's narrative essay? What new text would emerge by reading "Daisies" in the context of scholarly research? In other words, what new perspectives might develop from imposing Burke's "perspective by incongruity" (here, scholarship) on this personal form? In anticipation of the discussion of teaching strategies in chapter 5, I want to demonstrate how scholars can use academic evidence and personal evidence to achieve an enriched surplus perspective.

Throughout "Daisies," Laird makes it clear that she knows the commonplaces of process writing pedagogy. After noting the grade of ninety-five atop her husband's otherwise unmarked short story, she asks with just a touch of irony, "How would this developing writer learn anything from the writing without detailed response from his teacher, the opportunity for 'deep' revision, and/or input from peer review?" (121). She then provides an admittedly "hyperbolic view of what I [an informed compositionist in the late 1990s] *might* have done" (122, emphasis in original).

Since the essay hinges on the pedagogy of response, I would like to suggest superimposing on "Daisies" some of the literature that underlies Laird's project. Citing this kind of research would add another dimension to the argument. For example, Chris Anson introduces his collection *Writing and Response: Theory, Practice, and Research* by observing that the "process of response . . . is so fundamental to human interaction that when it is short-circuited, whether by accident or design, the result can hardly be interpreted as anything but a loss to humanity" ("Introduction" 1). David Bleich's essay in the same volume explains how current response theory is consistent with and inherent in social theories of learning and writing. Laird's essay also conjures a number of other compositionists and their practices: Donald Murray's early writing process articles, Nancy Sommers's seminal article on teachers' comments, Kenneth Bruffee's and Peter Elbow's work on peer response (*Writing*), Don Daiker's work on the effect of praise. By giving voice to theorists whose work clearly grounds her own teaching and is the "common knowledge" of our discipline, Laird would intensify our understanding of her conflict as she confronts the positive outcome of a teacher's nonresponse. By the same token, the published research effectively loses some of its authority when pressed into the background of Laird's experience, nicely redistributing the balance of power between personal and theoretical evidence.

Further, Laird calls into question the view that teacher response is requisite to writing instruction and writing improvement by suggesting that under the right circumstances, the grade itself is a kind of response. Certainly our current scholarship on grades is confusing. On the one hand, we have students and even teachers in the role of students clamoring for grades, stating that "grades were essential for them to know where they stood in the class" (Anderson and Speck 22). On the other, we need only turn to *Lives on the Boundary* to appreciate the damage caused by grades when they are used to label and sort students. To complicate "Daisies," to foster a "perspective by incongruity," Laird might turn to the assessment literature or ask how her argument might be differently narrated had Mr. Lewis awarded the story, without commentary or response, a grade of 75.

Crucially, however, the essay hangs on the question of effects. The boy who received the ninety-five became the trial attorney who excelled in language skills. What is the effect of our grading and our response on the "youthful enthusiasm and emerging self-confidence" of developing writers? "Would this student have chosen the same path after a class with me?" Laird asks herself and all of us who follow the "common sense" wisdom of contemporary writing theory (124). For an answer, Laird might turn to researchers who study the effects of teacher comments on students' ability to revise and on their motivation. Those researchers have found that responses that reflect an angry or hypercritical teacher are unhelpful and destructive to student initiative, as are marginal symbols or brief rubber-stamped comments (Sommers, "Responding"; and, e.g., Hillocks 160–68; Straub; Griffin). Therefore, in addition to the potentially appropriative nature of teacher response, which Laird alludes to in "Daisies" and which was first brought to our attention by Sommers and by Brannon and Knoblauch, she could find support for Mr. Lewis's decision to grade but not to comment by exploring in more depth the debilitating effects of teacher comments. "Daisies" is a worthy candidate for the kinds of supplementarity I've been suggesting. The addition of scholarly discourse, with its implied skepticism, rigidity, explanatory compulsion, and desire for connections, could offer a number of assenting and dissenting voices that would add both information and complexity. Such an effort would enhance our appreciation of the essay's central argument by contributing to its irreconcilability—in the end we still don't know whether Mr. Lewis was right, but we understand just how much was riding on his lucky guess. Simultaneously, the academic orientation (which we often take too seriously for our own good), when juxtaposed with the narrative orientation of Laird's reverie, creates a new, context-laden, emotionally inflected orientation and way of reading that both locates the author's personal interests and provides a more comprehensive way for readers to encompass them.

Turning to Teaching

In this chapter, I have tried to explain and illustrate the intellectual integrity of experiential discourse. I have tried to show that in addition to its appeals to emotion and identification, personal experience can make logical appeals, which can be evaluated as evidence in academic writing. I have also tried to point out the problems and limits of validating experiential evidence and to illustrate how competing orientations might productively complicate an argument.

Today, many of us celebrate scholarly writers who have recognized the value of multiple orientations and the uses of surplus for making their arguments. However, for our students to take advantage of this moment, we need to teach them how to successfully enact personal academic prose. As with other rhetorical genres, we need to develop instructional methods to assist our students in crafting such arguments, and we likewise need to ensure that their understanding of this approach enables them to use it successfully in other classes in the university and, as appropriate, in their professional lives. In the next chapter, I suggest several ways to teach personal academic argument and pose some questions about its future in and outside university settings.

And so, Michelle (or Mike or Devin or Robert) and I sit side by side at my office desk. My student is writing an academic argument about Louise Erdrich's "Skunk Dreams" (or Pennsylvania Dutch dialect differences or George Bush's rhetoric of war). "Do you mean that I can leave this part about my family (or my encounters with cultural intolerance or my stint in the National Guard) in my essay?" this student asks, trusting and somehow not really trusting at the same time. "Yes," I say with some confidence, "you can write personal academic arguments. And I will show you how."

5 / Teaching Personal Academic Argument

In my rhetorical theory class, my students are talking with me about the use of personal experience in their academic essays. Unlike Michelle's first-year composition class, which has always been a site of challenge and experimentation for me, this is an upper-division class, and I am preparing professional writing majors to compose for business, industry, or graduate school. We are in the middle of a discussion about genres, conventions, and the rhetorics of advertising, popular journalism, and essay prose.

"Could we use personal experience in Dr. Faulkner's Arthurian legends class?" Dan asks.

"Sure," Meredith responds, "Dr. Faulkner is crazy, so she'll let you try anything."

"What about Dr. Goodman's multicultural literature course?" they posit. "Would she let us do it?"

I explain that, for sure, Dr. Goodman would allow for personal discourse conventions but would want her students to be self-conscious about their efforts, to foreground their strategies and purposes so that readers could understand what they were up to. Then I stop to consider whether my students could actually bring it off. Do they know how to use personal writing well enough to make it work?

If students can produce effective prose that meets the course requirements and answers the questions that need to be answered, some teachers might be persuaded to permit genre blurring for writing about scholarly issues. In this chapter I offer suggestions for teaching personal academic argument based on strategies and assignments that I have used in my first-year writing courses, including the class in which I taught Michelle. I describe two central approaches, one for working with students who begin with experience-based essays and the other to introduce personal evidence to students writing academic discourse. For each approach, I offer a number of illustrative student samples and discuss students' efforts to blend the personal and academic. But first I present some general considerations for the kind of first-year writing instruction that I have in mind.

Instructional Considerations

In my first-year writing classes, readings, discussion, and writing assignments revolve around a central course theme, an issue that will invite not only personal meditation but also an array of popular or scholarly journal articles, such as the question of community, the meaning of "home," and the value of change. Thus, when the course addressed the construction of personal identity, we began the semester by discussing early childhood, as recaptured in memories, and investigated the self-concepts shaped by those memories. The readings about that issue included Judith Cofer's "Silent Dancing," Jamaica Kinkaid's "Biography of a Dress," Gary Soto's "The Childhood Worries, or Why I Became a Writer," and Elizabeth Stone's "Family Myths: Explanation Myths."[1] At another time, we interrogated the role of parents and family in the shaping of values and self-definition. An early set of course readings combined personal narratives, such as Raymond Carver's "My Father's Life" and Alice Walker's "Beauty: When the Other Dancer Is the Self," with more scholarly articles, such as David Elkind's "The Child Inside" and Susan Newby Short's "The Whispering of the Walls." Regardless of the course's theme, by using readings that encompass a range of genres, I hope to complicate my students' thinking about the issues we are discussing and to provide them with an array of discursive models as they determine how best to set forth their own arguments.

Judith Summerfield observes that narratives, often labeled "personal essays," are usually assigned at the beginning of a writing course because instructors incorrectly assume that "students can write easily, 'naturally,' without much thought, about what has happened to them" and that such assignments are therefore often "presented uncritically and unproblematically" (182). Because, like Summerfield, I view the inclusion of the personal as complex and, further, because I understand that when writing outside the composition classroom, one's content will usually dictate the document's form, I leave the choice of genre to my students. They decide, first, what to write about; next, how to construct their arguments; then, how much personal or academic discourse is called for. Throughout the semester, I design assignments to invite a range of strategies and genres, and I teach students to select evidence and methods appropriate to their projects' particular goals, intentions, and purposes. For any given essay project, students may choose to construct a narrative, a personal essay, or a more traditionally academic argument.

In one class, we had been discussing the influence of the media on viewers' attitudes, values, and behaviors. The assignment asked students to choose from six possible prompts, including these two, which I derived from suggested questions for readers in the course text, Donald McQuade and Robert Atwan's *The Writer's Presence* (pp. 699 and 609, respectively):

> *Prompt 1:* According to John Grisham's "Unnatural Killers," the media are to blame for much of the violence in our society. But homicide was a fact of American life long before movies or television. In fact, humans have always tried to blame inappropriate or bad behavior on outside influences. Briefly reflect on the argument Grisham is making; then, in several paragraphs, discuss other kinds of outside influences that people point to as blame for negative forms of social behavior. (Make your own position clear to your readers by showing whether you agree or disagree with these attributive causes.)
>
> *Prompt 2:* In her essay, "TV Addiction," Marie Winn compares television watching to drug and alcohol addictions. Select some other form of social or personal addiction (either serious or humorous but not X-rated, please) and use Winn's criteria to examine it. At the outset, make it clear

to your reader that you are basing your discussion on Winn's essay. Use quotes from real people, as Winn does. In the end, try to come to a meaningful (or funny, if appropriate) conclusion about this addiction.

Although the first prompt seems to call for a more outwardly focused analysis while the second invites multiple possibilities, including narrative, students in my classes know that they have the liberty to experiment, and I have never prohibited alternative formats and strategies. Using the Grisham prompt, students have written personal narratives to argue for the negative impact of computer games on children's developing social skills; using the Winn prompt, they've written academic arguments about the ubiquity of cell phones among teens. The range and types of readings and the specific demands of the related prompts ensure that students will vary their methods. In all the years that I have used this semester-long approach, no student has written, say, only personal narratives, because their handling of topics demands other genres (although many students tell me that they *wished* that they could write only personal narratives throughout the semester).

The prompts are simply suggestions for moving students toward a significant issue. I encourage them to limit and modify the topics according to their own needs and intentions, just as they are encouraged to find their best way to explain and support their arguments. Because I use a portfolio system for grading, drafts of selected essays are changed over time as the writer's perspective is reshaped by other readings, their writing group's insights, class conversations, and my written responses. By asking students to refer to their readings as source essays, I hope to complicate their writing and to demonstrate the value of engaging relevant writers in their conversations.

I teach the personal narrative not as an isolated unit but as a particular genre of writing, with its own conventions, like the other kinds of writing my students will be learning during the semester. In keeping with a specific genre, I stress that every act of writing is purposeful, and I make much of the fact that writers rarely produce finished drafts for themselves alone, with no other purpose than its composition. Initially, I use terms like *central idea, purpose,* and *point,* rather than *thesis,* to emphasize the range of purposes and structures available to writers. I want to diminish for them the limits and constraints of high school writing requirements, where even today, my students have learned in lockstep to reproduce the five-paragraph theme.

Students who have had difficulty in high school English classes often tell me how much they enjoy reflecting on and writing about their lives, families, and past events. When they write about these incidents and people, they find their expression easier and more relaxed, so that the idea of writing itself feels less threatening. Many of my students have never been permitted to write personal narratives or to use extended personal examples in high school, and my encouragement for them to do so often becomes one of the new freedoms they associate with college life. But they need to understand that personal essays, like all writing, are intended for others and, as such, are not simply an exercise in emotion or facile moral lessons imposed didactically for the reader's edification.

Finally, we must be cautious when we solicit from students essays of disclosure. As the samples indicate, I carefully construct assignment prompts so as not to require ultrarevealing narratives. Of course, there are occasions when students may find confessional or disclosive episodes particularly effective, and as Anne Ruggles Gere has recently shown, a studied choreography of silence and disclosure can produce aesthetically, ethically, and politically powerful personal writing.

Approaching Personal Academic Arguments

Here I describe two central orientations to teach students to develop their skills as writers of personal academic discourse. One way helps them to incorporate more academic conventions of paraphrase and quotation into personal essays (both personal narratives of experience and personal essays of the Montaigne variety), as in my imaginary revision of Ellen A. Laird's "Daisies"; the other shows them how to build appropriate personal reference into more academic essays where sources are involved, as in my responses to Michelle. Although I separate these strategies for purposes of discussion, in my classes, options continue to intersect and my recommendations to any student are specific to the text already written, the stage of the draft, and the time of semester.

With either orientation, I help students to understand the benefits derived from supplementing the personal and academic worldviews within the same text. In my classes, I borrow from both Kenneth Burke and Walter Fisher to describe ways of thinking associated with the scientific and narrative orientations as we discuss such questions as "Where do we get our values?" "How do we agree on what is meaningful?" "In what kinds of communities do we participate?" Usually such questions and the related notion that we perceive the world from a number of structurally mediated perspectives intersect with readings or occur in the context of students' essays, but I also talk about academic and narrative orientations when I explain particular genre expectations and conventions.

Most often, however, students come to understand how to work within and how to benefit from these competing orientations through my responses to their papers in conference or in written comments on their drafts. This kind of "reorienting" is, thus, more a process of revision than it is direct instruction. Also, during peer writing group sessions, I will suggest that peer group members help writers to find places in their drafts that seem to invite an alternate discourse, perhaps an abstract discussion in need of a personal example or an experiential account in need of a secondary source. Naturally, reorientations in a writer's thinking and changes in perspective are subtle, which means that the work of the draft and the student's reenvisioning of the project will occur by degrees. More accomplished writers often know instinctively when the personal is called for (just as they know when a citation is called for), but part of the task of teaching writing is to introduce new strategies and genres to the students' repertoires, perhaps even suggesting ways of writing that they had not yet imagined.

Starting from the Personal

It is probably unsurprising that students often start the semester by framing their arguments as experience-based essays. Likewise unremarkable, they typically choose to use a published personal narrative from our readings, rather than a scholarly essay, as their required "source" evidence. As student writers grapple with the demands of writing and their own, often ambivalent, perspectives on topical issues, the published narratives are obviously more accessible and apparently more pliable for supporting their emergent arguments. To teach them how to blend genres, I take advantage of this inclination and build it into early assignments. Then I arrange assignments sequentially to foster a greater appreciation of the ways an academic conversation can be brought to a personal text.

To explain the first stage of my instructional process, I will describe the work of one student, Chad. In an early personal essay, Chad argued that parents are only one factor among many to influence a child's developing identity. He asserted, "You have your teachers, religious figures, friends and parents or guardians[, but] wherever you gain your values they will always be with you in some aspect of your life." Chad used a number of hypothetical examples to examine the ways that economics, social class, parents, and peers contribute to a child's developing values and to emphasize the difficulties of changing deeply entrenched patterns of belief later in life. Toward the end of his essay, he discussed his own family's expectations, emphasizing the soundness of his parents' instruction and their sustained influence on his thinking, and he presented illustrative personal examples to support his claims that "the way you were brought up is the same way, roughly, that you will raise your kids. You may find yourself acting or doing the same things your parents did." He wrote, "[F]rom my parents I have learned to work hard and conserve the money I earn; it doesn't just get handed to me," explaining that he and his parents shared the cost of purchasing his first truck and that they gave him full responsibility for its maintenance. When I read Chad's essay, his example, intended to emphasize the tenacity of values training, seemed too celebratory and unreflective, and so I suggested that he fulfill our essay requirement for "at least one source" by considering whether parental influence was always beneficial.

As a result, Chad's next draft referred to Raymond Carver's "My Father's Life," which served as additional evidence for his claims. He wrote that Carver's father

> was always moving from place to place . . . [and] had a drinking problem. [Likewise, a]s Carver grew older and had a family, he found himself moving and drinking a lot also. . . . It ended up that he had become in certain ways his father, even though he vowed not to be.

In this draft, Chad did not yet interrogate values as products of social factors (although he did attempt to articulate a relationship among family income, parental presence in the home, and the mediating effects of television and older siblings). Further, he did not use his "source" essay as scholarship but rather cast Raymond Carver as a person whose lived experience, like Chad's own, exemplified parental effects.

Many of my developing writers start out this way, choosing as evidence the personal narratives that they've enjoyed reading and discussing in class. I view this choice as an early kind of source engagement, a mechanism for students to see how the work of others may contribute to their arguments and a way to complicate their all-to-easy claims to the validity of their personal opinions. Thus, when Joanne, another student in the same class, wrote in her essay on the same topic, "Parents always try to do what is best for their children," I encouraged her to include Carver's essay among her sources. Recognizing Carver's struggle with and against his family's dynamics and his ultimate allegiance to his father's name challenged Joanne's unreflective tribute to her parents' child-rearing skills, at least to the degree that she tempered her claims about what "all parents do."

As students begin to relate to source texts, as Chad did, to recognize in their readings both identification and difference, I encourage them to clarify and understand difficult material by provisionally interpreting arguments in terms of their own experiences. Here

I borrow from Spellmeyer's point that much writing instruction in academic discourse forces students to accommodate the formal features of genre without adequate understanding of the subject matter. Spellmeyer views personal writing as a way to help students to find the common ground between their own perspectives and those of more established scholars. To help them engage with their source's ideas, I sometimes ask students to "collaborate" with one or more of the authors we are reading by drawing from their own observations and experiences as well as their sources' as they analyze or engage textual arguments.

Vanessa's essay illustrates the kind of weaving between source and personal that I hope for at this stage of my students' development. After a class discussion of Richard Rodriguez's "Aria" in *Hunger of Memory,* Vanessa wrote about the intimacy of family language, its seduction, and its pitfalls. Her analysis moves between Rodriguez's personal narrative and her own to explain that

> like Rodriguez, I have come to miss the familiarity of intimate conversation since I moved away from home. In his case, he could not use his intimate family language while in the public eye. I cannot use my family language as I talk among the new friends and acquaintances that I have found since my move.

Further on, she uses examples of her family's "private language" to illuminate the relationship between language and culture, finding, like Rodriguez, a positive coupling of speech sounds and domestic comfort.

> At school in the cafeteria, there is a harsh loud hustle where all of the words blend together into a mass of soundless confusion. Rodriguez also experienced the same crowd of words as he walked along the street of the city. To escape from the confusion Rodriguez turned to home where he could listen to the soothing sounds of family. I find comfort at home when I speak of the day-to-day occurrences that make farm

life and conversation rewarding. I feel a sense of assurance as I tell my *daad* (dad) a story about a *caaf* (calf) that was just born in our barn. He takes a *sip* or *swaller* (drink) of his *pop* (soda) and we head out the door to the truck to check on the new *caaf.*

While Vanessa agrees with Rodriguez that family language offers refuge, she rejects his notion that private language must be silenced for one to become a public-speaking citizen. Unlike Rodriguez, Vanessa finds in the language of home the unconditional acceptance and positive reinforcement that give confidence to one's public voice.

In Vanessa's essay, personal experience provided additional evidence that both confirmed and denied arguments in the source text; it also enabled her to carve her own argument, to make a place for herself as an academic speaker, and it opened a space for further analysis, research, and study, especially in regard to the cultural configurations that make her view of public and private language so different from Richard Rodriguez's. In my follow-up comments to Vanessa, I suggested that she next interrogate her claims by examining the arguments of language theorists and others who write about the relationship among power, oppression, and particular discourses or dialects. But I also reminded Vanessa that as she extended her analysis, she could continue to invoke as evidence relevant personal narratives and examples.

As students become adept at using personal experience in more sophisticated and nuanced ways, I use prompts like the following:

> Discuss why you think that memories from childhood continue to influence, to haunt, many people even as they grow older and move away from their immediate families. Refer to your own experiences and observations as well as to our readings in order to provide evidence for your explanation.

Requesting balance among personal and scholarly evidence teaches that source information should be not simply adjunct to the writer's arguments but intrinsic to their primary considerations. In the case of James, I faced a sophisticated thinker who needed to understand the intimate relationship between his own experiences and theories expressed in the texts he was reading. To develop his argument that the impact of early experience is repeatedly revised in light of new knowledge, although childhood memories are more forceful and tenacious because there is nothing to work against them, I suggested he make greater use of his sources.

James's strategy was to try to recapture his initial childhood response to two significant events, then to revisit these events from the distance of years. He wanted to explain how his memories had been "smoothed out" over time, such that new insights had blended with these first impressions, changing their impact and their significance. In the first scene, set in a summer resort town when he was five or six years old, James recalls a fight between "two very angry guys . . . over some girl." In the second scene, he comes upon his father digging a grave for the family cat and "remember[s] the outline of the cat's body underneath the blanket." These childhood scenes become not moments of epiphany but rather "imprints" that initiate opportunities for more mature insights in later life.

James had been learning to incorporate published research in the same ways I've already described. At this point, it was important that I encourage him to use his source texts as a bridging strategy to expand and develop his arguments. I didn't want him to merely announce similarities between his and his source authors' childhood experiences (as Vanessa did when reflecting on Rodriguez); rather I wanted to show him how to use source texts to extend his central position. James selected Eudora Welty's "The Little Store" to fulfill his source requirement, and in conference we discussed how Welty's worldview changed after her encounter with the "monkey man." In his next draft, James referred to this scene as he explained, "Young Welty begins to see [that] there is more to the little store than she ever noticed before. . . . She sees there is more to the world than just herself." Rather than comparing himself to Welty, he describes Welty's emergent understanding, allowing Welty's insights to theorize his own. When, in James's final para-

graphs, he leaps to the present day, characterizing his adult responses to fights between young men or cat burials, he can effectively make this move because has used his source material to partially construct his argument.

The sequence of assignment strategies I have just outlined as-
sists students to integrate academic materials into their personal
essays. With intervention and instruction, the inclusion of an alternate perspective should propel shifts and turns in their thinking.
In the discussion below, I take the opposite approach, starting with
academic essays to include personal evidence. My goal, however, is
the same: the development of personal academic arguments. In that
regard, despite the genre from which they initially spring, later drafts
of students' essay will seem generically similar.

Starting from the Academic

The inclusion of personal experience in academic writing
supplements (in the broader sense of addition and modification)
how students imagine, understand, and write about their particular topics, but it also helps to demystify scholarly research. Novice
writers often endow published texts with unshakable authority,
which is why so many students think research is an activity in cut-
ting and pasting. Few understand that such work requires active
engagement with texts-as-interlocutors. We can teach students to
engage by encouraging them to place their experiential evidence
within the contexts of the texts they are reading and to look at the
ways all of these perspectives oppose, modify, and reinforce each
other. Here, again, my approach is sequential; I encourage students
to write increasingly more complicated essays by bringing their
personal experiences to bear on their interrogation of source texts.

Justin's essay "Television Families" illustrates one student's
early-in-the-semester effort to use personal experience to counter
a source or to strengthen a claim. Justin had originally focused on
Marie Winn's "Television and Family Rituals," one of several articles
we had read to explore the impact of media on the social construction of personal identity. To begin, Justin had summarized Winn's
historical account of the ubiquity of television in the American

home. He identified as central to Winn's concerns the loss of family rituals (which he defined, paraphrasing Winn, as "common happenings within a family that draw family members together and help give them a separate identity from other families"). Allying himself with Winn, he conceded that "very few family rituals have defeated the television set." In our class discussion, Justin, along with several other students, had resisted Winn, calling her "reactionary" and "unwilling to change with the times." They had argued that television viewing, like other media activities, had become a bonding event in itself, and that Winn's definition of *ritual* was too narrow. However, when it came time to write and Justin was face-to-face with the published text, he found it difficult to counter Winn's assertions.

To help Justin resist the authority in Winn's essay, I suggested that he examine his own family's rituals, both those that involved television watching and those involving activities away from the TV set. The next draft went far afield, with Justin's describing several of his family's rituals in vivid detail. Yet through this exercise, he began to place Winn's arguments in a different context. On the basis of an investigation into his family's practices, he revised his essay to argue that in itself, television viewing is not more or less detrimental to family relationships; rather the emotional health of the family is dependent on the desire of family members to create new rituals and develop new ways of "showing our togetherness." He describes the aftermath of Thanksgiving dinner, when family members "congregate towards the living room to watch the football games." He stresses that "while [his relatives] are engrossed in the game, they still manage to converse . . . [and] make time to talk among themselves." Likewise, he writes, "[O]n Christmas Eve night while the snow comes down, my mother, sister, and I cuddle up on the couch to watch *A Christmas Carol,* the movie that has become part of our Christmas tradition." In his closing remarks, Justin speculates that perhaps "only dysfunctional families fall apart due to television." Ultimately, he suggests that "television should not decompose our family bonds; instead we should use it to our advantage to create new rituals and to strengthen many of the old ones."

Critics may contend that there is no way to counter Justin's claim that his family has found a way to make television a part of their tradition rather than an impediment to it, and, of course, they will be right. But by arguing with Winn in the context of his experience, Justin was able to demystify his source while still positioning Winn's argument respectfully within his own. Further, juxtaposing his evidence against Winn's major research enabled him to grasp the specificity and limits of his assertions. He saw his evidence as the exception to the rule and therefore as a way to complicate the arguments in Winn's text without overturning them.

In Justin's essay, personal experience operated as a counterweight to Winn's argument, and much of his essay was taken up with establishing the cogency and the authority of his evidence. The next step involves teaching students to balance various kinds of evidence, including their personal observations, and assisting them in teasing out the ways that their epistemological positions clash and blend. To accomplish these tasks, I ask students to use additional textual research and personal evidence to revisit topics that they've already written about or have shown some interest in during the semester. Shawn, whose essay I describe below, had written an early academic argument about the "problem" of divorce. In this later essay on the impact of divorce on children, he continued his research, using Judith Wallerstein and Sandra Blakeslee's "On the Brow of the Hill," which discusses the damaging impact of divorce on women and children; David Elkind's article "The Child Inside," which analyzes contemporary social factors that force children to assume adult roles; and Tillie Olsen's short story "I Stand Here Ironing," which Shawn acknowledged as fiction but found relevant to his argument.

To achieve the balance that I'd been encouraging in class, Shawn supplemented his sources with personal illustrations, centrally contrasting changes in his family's structure, emotional stability, and lifestyle before and after his father's departure. He began his essay by citing Wallerstein and Blakeslee but moved quickly to reconstruct a story of financial change and subsequent economic uncertainty.

> Prior to my parents' divorce, my family was supported
> solely by my dad. He worked about fifty hours a week,
> making nearly twenty dollars an hour at an aluminum plant
> in Lancaster, Pennsylvania. Furthermore, he would bring
> home another couple hundred dollars a week from winning
> billiard tournaments at the local pool hall. The money he
> brought home was more than enough to support a relatively
> small family of four.

Shawn's personal account continues for another paragraph, as he
describes the difficulties imposed by his father's departure.

> Facing the impossible task of being a full time mother and
> holding a full time job, my mother was forced to enter the
> working world inexperienced and naïve. It was hard on her
> physically and emotionally, not to mention that it was
> equally hard on my sister and me.

He next invokes Olsen's narrative as evidence for his argument,
explaining, "my mother, like Emily's mother, found it difficult to
work full time and still share a sufficient amount of time with her
children."

When Shawn told me that he was going to use Elkind's research
about the negative effects of contemporary social conditions on the
normal developmental processes of children and adolescents, I
wasn't sure how he was going to make relevant connections. But he
explained that in his view, divorce, like other situations that Elkind
mentions, "force[s] children to grow up too quickly." Drawing from
his own experience, Shawn knew that when a single parent is both
caregiver and wage earner and when family finances are insufficient
to mediate these demands, older children (like Shawn himself) will
be expected to assume responsibility for child care of younger siblings, household maintenance, and economic contributions. Therefore I tried to guide Shawn to cite, summarize, and explain his research and, at the same time, to reflect on his personal insights,

threading them through at appropriate locations in his essay. Using personal experience in this way helped Shawn to contextualize his authorities without giving way to a purely personal narrative or privileging personal knowledge over academic analysis. Supplementing a personal or academic orientation should lead to surplus, contradictions that cannot be contained within the neat confines of the traditional essay. The final step in this instructional process, therefore, is to help students to live with uncertainty and irreconcilability in their writing, even as they seek quick closure and easy answers. We can do so by teaching about competing orientations, providing Walter Fisher's or Kenneth Burke's vocabulary (e.g., the narrative paradigm, the rational world paradigm) to encompass these concepts. Crucially, we can encourage students to look for these surplus possibilities in their own writing, to find places where the academic and personal might intersect, lead in different directions or in no direction. Such encouragement is just what I tried to offer when Shawn invoked Elkind's research on teenage suicides to support his claim that "along with financial troubles, many children of divorced families suffer emotionally under the weight of divorce."

Quoting Elkind's finding that "the stresses of growing up fast often result in troubled and troublesome behavior during adolescence" (328), Shawn made an enthymemic leap, asserting that with increases in divorce, among other pressures, "[i]t is no shock that drug use among teens is on the uprise." But there were problems with coherence as soon as Shawn reintroduced his own story, which tells of children who did not turn to drugs, who did in fact grow up to become responsible adults. While Shawn attempted a logical explanation, suggesting that perhaps "[m]y parents divorced when I was too young to realize what was happening or for that matter to even care what was happening [and] therefore I did not have to use drugs to take away the pain," I pointed out that age seven was certainly old enough to have recognized and been affected by one's parents' divorce. We agreed that the narrative paradigm of his and Olsen's stories allowed for paradox, contradiction, and mitigating circumstance but that the rational paradigm required greater interrogation of the issues or conditions that surround children in single-parent families. To reconcile competing orientations, we said, Shawn would need to deepen his theory, review more sources, and consider how he might rewrite his understanding of his experience.

By the same token, I was delighted with Shawn's strategy for closing his essay and ultimately encouraged him to leave his concluding discussion unresolved. He writes,

> It is true that children are forced to grow up faster now for many reasons, and it is obvious to me that divorce is one of them. I am not attempting to condemn divorce because many divorces are justified with relevant reasoning; however, I do think married couples with children should consider the pain they are going to cause themselves and more importantly the pain they are going to cause their children.

To be sure, there are many things I could have said to Shawn as he further revised this draft. However, as his teacher, I thought it was important not to force him to reconcile completely his competing observations and claims. In a different but not unrelated context, Susan Wells speaks of the compulsion among writing teachers to resolve discontinuities in our students' writing. Both the giving and taking of assertion, of "truth," and of the unitary "presence" of the writer within the text should be not reconciled but rather celebrated. Referring to a student essay that "represents [this] doubleness of the speaker and language that is implicit in writing," Wells says, "This piece of writing does not need to be saved . . . ; rather we need to save ourselves from the requirement that such writing become single, unitary, 'coherent'" ("Doubleness" 122–23). It is, in fact, the sophisticated threading of narrative and academic perspectives and the resultant absence of closure in Shawn's account that I want to celebrate.

Learning to Construct Subjects and Experiences

As we teach students how to supplement their varied discourses, we must also teach them that personal writing is not a reflection of a true, authentic self but is a representation of the most appropriate version of a writer for a particular text. We can teach them the rhetoric of voice and ethical appeal, not to suggest that they mislead readers or misrepresent themselves but that they choose as all writers do and play at and with subject positions. By disrupting the illusion of a "real, authentic, stable self," Judith Summerfield explains, we can promote an understanding of

> who we can be as writers and the . . . writerly possibilities that arise out of considering multiple perspectives and voices, multiple versions and truths. We can offer students the enabling notion that, even in their autobiographical writings, the narrator is a stance, a perspective, an angle, in this version, this representation, and not the student confessing his or her authentic feelings or truths. (187)

Most first-year students are unaware of the ways in which they might foreground their narrator's character, knowledge, and goodwill to foster greater confidence and respect for their academic arguments or to use the narrator construct to adopt, subvert, reject, or attack particular articulations of meaning. It is therefore helpful for them to see such strategies "in action" in the course readings or in sample essays. Sometimes I ask students to characterize a writer whose essay or article we have just read, basing their description on the text itself rather than on what they might already know about the person. I offer suggestions for qualities they might consider: Is the writer intelligent? Fair? Honest? Willing to explain? Self-serious? And so on. Naturally, it's easier to find these traits in personal essays, so narratives like Russell Baker's "Gumption" are a good starting point. Political speeches also serve well for this kind of activity. For example, recently, I brought in several of President George W. Bush's addresses that followed September 11, and we talked about how the speaker was representing himself in the various texts and why he might choose a particular stance within a specific context. With current political texts, students can picture a real audience and appreciate more directly the speaker's interest in building a relationship with that audience. When we look at academic texts, such as educational research or social science articles, we also consider how a writer persuades us that she knows her subject or that he has "done his homework" and whether we actually like this person. It's also important to talk about what the various texts "give away," that is, what we discern that is not apparently intended.

While these activities teach about the writer's implied character, helping students to separate the writer from the narrator is crucial if we want them to read texts more critically (for example, to understand the difference between how we are positioned by and through our culture and how we choose to position ourselves within texts) and if we want students to appreciate their own rhetorical options. I have used two essays from Barbara Kingsolver's *High Tide in Tucson* to make this issue a little clearer. In "Stone Soup," Kingsolver mixes personal narrative, illustrative example, commentary, and scholarly research to argue that Americans should embrace a broader definition of *family* than has traditionally been accepted by cultural norms. Because the voice in the text is highly inflected, students have little difficulty characterizing the narrator, whom they take to be the writer. We then read "In Case You Ever Want to Go Home Again," for both its representation of the narrator and its deliberate efforts to place autobiographical "truth" in doubt. Kingsolver describes how, in returning to her hometown as a celebrated writer, she rewrites history as she signs autographs for the high school heroes who had rejected her as a teenager by writing "long, florid inscriptions referring to our great friendship in days gone by" (42). The students quickly see differences in the textual voices, and they appreciate that writers make choices about how they want to represent themselves. But the more important point I want to help them to see is that no representation of themselves is the "real" one, although they have at their disposal various strategies for constructing assorted, even contradictory, selves across the page.

To translate this understanding to their own writing, students need opportunities to write from different standpoints and subject positions. Wells suggests exercises that range from "simple role-playing, the requirement to speak *as if* one were a lab technician, a researcher, a character in a story" to those that invite "exaggerated, counterfactual, and consciously deceptive assignments," which ultimately turn to ethical questions about evidence and documentation ("Doubleness" 119). Wells stresses that students need such opportunities to reenact in quite deliberate ways the multivoicedness of all writing. Moreover, in writing from different subject positions, students may be able to view the world from vantage points they had not heretofore imagined.

Several years ago, I wrote an article about a student who, without my knowledge, submitted an essay that did just that. Carla's personal narrative traced her emotional development when, at age sixteen, her mother died, leaving her to care for younger siblings and a grieving father. Suddenly, she faced endless responsibilities that included laundry, meal preparation, and housecleaning, in addition to completing her own schoolwork and trying, fruitlessly, to maintain peer friendships. Toward the end of her essay, Carla observed that while she'd once been a carefree teen whose only concerns were "cars, boys, and looking good," she had come to understand and appreciate what she had formerly taken for granted. The punch line occurred long after the essay was graded, when it became clear that Carla actually lived in an affluent, two-parent family and her central concerns were "cars, boys, and looking good."

Because neither her peer group members nor I knew that the essay was fiction, however, our questions and suggestions were aimed at helping the narrator to further interrogate and develop her existing draft.[2] Without our realizing it, I think we were encouraging Carla to analyze her fictive situation from an alternative discursive perspective. Perhaps by giving herself "permission to lie" (Wells, "Doubleness" 121), in some measure, Carla felt what it was like to actually be the female head of household, a surrogate mother, at age seventeen. I cannot say that for sure. What I do know is that in her development as a writer, Carla was able to produce vivid and believable prose.[3]

While Carla's essay demonstrates how students might be encouraged to play at various narrator roles as a lesson in subject performance, I acknowledge that her fabrication raises serious questions about the use of personal experience *as* evidence, and as Wells suggests, if we are going to encourage students to fictionalize, we are likewise going to need to address the ethics of fictional representation. As I discussed earlier, the issues are quite complicated and involve at least some of the following considerations: the power and efficacy of constructed evidence to the argument at hand as well as the reader's assumptions about the text, the writer's autobiographical "contract" (even in a minimal form), the question of deception, and the question of who might be hurt or diminished by the fictive representation. In courses that include essay writing, autobiography and memoir, creative nonfiction, or journalism, it is fitting that ethical issues are examined (B. Williams). Likewise, when we teach students to use their personal experiences as evidence for academic argument, we need to be sure they understand what is at stake in their representations.

Furthermore, after reading an earlier version of this manuscript, Bruce Ballenger astutely observed, "I wonder whether deliberate fabrication might lead students away from ambiguity and uncertainty and towards merely confirmation of what they already think." In other words, it is possible that by privileging story over memory, students might avoid the difficult task of examining the complexities of writing about lived experience. Given that the folding of experiential evidence into academic discourse is intended to expand and complicate, to produce competing narratives and overlapping meanings, writing instructors will need to probe, as they always have, the easy solution, the happy ending. At the same time, they might initiate class discussions of truth, memory, and representation with such essays as Lynn Bloom's "Living to Tell the Tale" and Bronwyn Williams's "Never Let the Truth Stand in the Way of a Good Story."

Still, it seems that for most of my students, the opposite situation is more common; they are convinced that in their personal accounts, they must tell "the whole truth and nothing but the truth," and as a result, teachers enter the minefield of evaluating lives instead of texts. Further, they lose opportunities to talk about the construction of experience as a rhetorical strategy, to make a place and a practice for filling in the gaps of memory, as I did with Mike in chapter 3. Summerfield stresses this "crucial distinction" between the life and the text, urging teachers

> to distinguish . . . the events being represented, the "what happened," from the procedures representing what happened—the textual options. . . . To distinguish event from discourse is to respect the confusions, mutabilities, shifts, and needs of memory, to problematize memory. (183)

In other words, we need to demonstrate clearly and explicitly how the personal can be rhetorical.

From a related angle, students can be guided to evaluate personal experience offered as evidence in published essays and articles. We can help them to determine the commonplaces and assumptions relied upon, the work's narrative probability and narrative fidelity, as I did with Ellen Laird's and Raymond Carver's essays. Portions of Ruth Behar's autobiographical ethnography *The Vulnerable Observer* work well in this kind of exercise because they are provocative and revealing as well as evidential. Students might also engage Jane Tompkins's "Me and My Shadow," which excites questions not only about the validity of evidence but also about whose evidence can "count."[4] Likewise, many students appreciate Nancy Sommers's "Between the Drafts" because they can identify with her argument even as they appraise the efficacy of her personal evidence. But students also benefit from reading and evaluating blurred genre writing by less acclaimed writers. With appropriate permission, strong student essays like Michelle's "Nature's Lessons" make wonderful samples for assessing experience-based claims and evidence.

Personal Experience in Public Writing

Throughout this book, I have been urging a new configuration of academic prose that blends personal experience and academic argument to arrive at alternative modes of understanding. But composition teaching today is also moving in a different direction, focusing on writing that has a more significant impact in the public space beyond the classroom. Christian R. Weisser explains that the goal of such instruction is "written discourse that attempts to engage an audience of local, regional, or national groups or individuals in order to bring about progressive societal change" (90). Although we most often associate public writing instruction with service-learning projects, according to Weisser, students can participate in a number of arenas where their writing will be socially useful and politically active. In addition to writing documents for nonprofit agencies, Weisser sees opportunities for students to learn public forms of writing by way of community outreach, public service projects, Internet chat rooms and Web writing, cross-institutional paired writing assignments, oral history collections, and adult literacy programs (Wells, "Rogue"; Ward; Herzberg; Grobman, "(Re)Writing"). While composition teachers have expressed extraordinary support for public-directed writing instruction, its attendant texts seem distant from personal discourse. Nevertheless, I suggest that experiential evidence has a place in public writing and in the work that surrounds the teaching of these discourses.

Because, for its strongest advocates, public writing instruction is political, aimed at addressing injustice and solving social problems, it requires analysis and reflection as well as action. Because such writing is directed at the lived experiences of individuals, groups, and communities, understanding comes by way of participating in, as well as interrogating, public contexts. This intimate relationship between practice and theory, between action and reflection distinguishes service-learning as a pedagogic strategy (Deans 2). Reflection, often by way of journals or in classroom discussions, invites students to consider not only what they've done or seen but what it means. In the three models of service-learning described by Thomas Deans, service-learners reflect on their experiences in different ways.

In writing-for-the-community courses, students partner with local agencies to produce needed documents, like grant proposals and brochures (53), and as such use public discourse in professional documents. In the case study Deans describes, however, students used personal writing to reflect on ethical and civic issues; these reflections concentrated on "the learning process, on community needs, and on personal rewards" (79). Although Deans asserts that the "writing for" paradigm is least likely to foster cultural critique than other models, it seems to me that naming one's experience may be an initial touchstone to critical consciousness, as it "encourages meaningful connections between school and society, knowledge and experience, and individual and community" (79–80).

In describing the writing-about-the-community model of service-learning, Deans explains that personal experiences become the texts to be analyzed and reflected upon in order to interrogate broader social issues. This approach is executed in Bruce Herzberg's expository writing classes at Bentley, where students tutor in local elementary schools and then critically analyze the themes of literacy and schooling, as such issues bear on their service. In Herzberg's approach, the students' experiences are the bridge to analytical writing, and personal writing is an intermediate reflective stage for question and critique.

Finally, Deans explains writing-with-the-community models in terms of the partnership between Carnegie Mellon University and Community House through the Community Literacy Center in Pittsburgh. In this case, university student mentors work with teens to draft published documents intended to "not simply critique or express, but also problem-solve, instigate social action, and intervene in the world" (120). Mentors also develop a research paper, called the inquiry project, a hybrid genre composed of multiple voices and discourses, based on their experience on site.

Depending on its ultimate publication venue, student service that involves collecting oral histories could be classified as either writing-for or writing-with the community. For a number of years, Gratz College in Philadelphia has sought volunteers to interview and record the stories of Holocaust survivors. Those oral testimonies are then archived for future research. Whether students participate in formal collections or engage in more local or classroom-based ethnographic initiatives, such work readily combines with academic research about historic contexts and social conditions. And these documents, I suggest, may be welcomed by community, religious, regional, or cultural groups that seek records. Thus, lived experience, the stories of others and the stories of self, may have significant value for serious scholarly or public documents.

Weisser, building on the work of Nancy Fraser and Wells, writes that classrooms also constitute public spaces or subaltern public spheres, especially when differences are confronted and contested. He suggests, following Wells, transinstitutional paired writing classes, a project I undertook by linking my first-year writing students at Penn State Berks, in east central Pennsylvania, with e-mail buddies in a first-year class at Columbus State University in western Georgia. Setting up weekly computer-lab "meetings," Professor Noreen Lape and I asked our students to discuss a number of shared course readings and to collaboratively write essays about Olsen's "I Stand Here Ironing." Over the semester, students on both campuses struggled to communicate and to understand perspectives mediated by differences resulting from (at least) class, race, and geography. In their e-mails, many students referred to incidents in their own lives and compared them with those of the narrator and her daughter and to relevant scholarly articles. This strategy allowed students to highlight differences in their experiences without directly disagreeing with their long-distance partners. The resulting documents revealed students' efforts to understand and negotiate conflicts in their disparate worldviews and readings. In this project and in their final collaborative essays, personal, academic, and more public discourses dramatically intersected.

On a more immediate level, classrooms can become public spheres involved in the analysis of public and counterpublic discourses (Wells, "Rogue" 338–39; Weisser 98–99). Using this approach, Weisser suggests, classes choose particular issues and examine associated public documents to determine "what voices have been heard and acknowledged, what voices have been marginalized, silenced, or excluded, and how discourse on particular issues has changed or developed as a result of larger political and social climates in which they've been generated" (98). In Wells's view, students and teachers should cultivate skills that include "an orientation toward performance rather than disclosure, and a broadened appreciation of performance inside and outside of texts" ("Rogue" 339). As a result, students will learn to identify and create effective but noncoercive forms of public advocacy ("Rogue" 339). The kinds of work Wells describes do not preclude observations, discussion, and assessment of the student's experience or of the lives of those involved, provided that experiential discourse is not used instrumentally for the purpose of unmediated or manipulative disclosure.

In arguing for the role of public writing instruction in composition studies, Weisser underscores the discipline's powerful social and political obligations. But he links these goals directly to real students and to their lived experiences. Weisser states,

> For many compositionists, the classroom—or, more specifically, the writing course—has emerged as a microcosm of the public sphere, as our point of contact with the "real" world out there somewhere. This point of contact is something that distinguishes composition from many of the academic disciplines; our close and personal connections with students differentiates our work from the "merely academic" pursuits of our colleagues down the hall. If we believe that power is entrenched in discourse and that language is an instrumental tool in shaping knowledge and reality, we could, by extension, assume that the work that we do can have tangible, immediate implications in the world. (91)

Weisser reminds us that the work of language, and thus of composition, is invariably political *and* personal. However, most proponents of public writing instruction are not urging the insertion of experiential evidence in public documents. Although popular discourse has shifted toward personal narrative, we will have to wait to see whether this shift applies to other kinds of public writing as well. In the meantime, students and teachers who seek to subvert discourses of power might test the waters of personal public discourse.

Starting Here

The blurred genre of personal academic argument is a fruitful discourse that should be tapped for composition research and taught in composition classrooms. Viewing personal writing as a construct enriches our understanding of its rhetorical potential while reducing anxiety about this discourse as an unmediated, coherent expression of a personal subject. Likewise, viewing experience as a reconstituted or fictive representation expands the possibilities for teaching and using experiential evidence, even as it acknowledges the complexities of those representations. To explain the logical processes and validation procedures for interrogating the rhetorical personal, I have introduced rhetorical theories, both classical and contemporary. The result of uniting personal and academic discourses is *surplus,* a new orientation that offers writers and readers an enlarged, complicated, and perhaps irreconcilable perspective. Finally, I have offered ways to teach personal academic argument: starting with personal writing and supplementing with source-based academic discourse and, alternatively, beginning with academic essays and supplementing with experience based evidence. Also, I have shown that personal academic argument can be an important tool in classrooms focused on more public forms of writing.

In academic settings, the use of personal experience as evidence remains highly controversial. As theorists and teachers of writing, we are rightfully concerned about the forms our discourse takes and about the kinds of discourse we teach because we know that our discursive choices both establish and enact our understanding of the world. When we ask about the relevance and suitability of lived experience in scholarly and student writing, we address larger questions about the status of subjects, the authenticity of experience, and the power of rhetoric. There are good reasons to invoke personal experience, and there are appropriate ways to do it while attending to pertinent philosophical and political considerations. If we understand why the personal "works" and how to use it effectively, we should appreciate the potential of personal academic argument.

Michelle's first-year composition class is long over. She has completed her sophomore writing requirement, "Writing in the Social Sciences," has tutored basic writers, and has led developmental writing groups. Now a junior at another university, majoring in public relations and minoring in journalism, she tells me by e-mail that she hopes to obtain a summer internship with a local newspaper. Over the years, Michelle has effectively rehearsed and occupied myriad discourses, including personal, academic, public, and professional. Like most writers, Michelle understands genre conventions; she makes choices and determines which kinds of evidence are appropriate to particular kinds of writing. On some occasions, she recognizes that personal experience is called for and knows that her examples and narratives make a logical case, are evidentially sound, and are ultimately persuasive. She can select her stories, bring them to life, and connect with her readers and with academic texts because she's had freedom (as well as training) to consider narrative and rational orientations and to practice written forms in which perspectives clash and blend.

These are just the writerly opportunities we should be offering all our students. They are also the writerly opportunities we should be offering ourselves.

Appendix

Notes

Works Cited

Index

Appendix

"Nature's Lessons" by Michelle Grider

The wind whistles through the arriving spring air. At the same moment, a beautiful doe is entering into this world, while the sound of birds chirping can be heard floating through the thawing air. A wonderful beginning to a story you think. Yes, this could be fiction, but in reality it is life for the nature cycle. People seem to be going through life not realizing what is around them. Day after day, year after year, people go along with the hustle and bustle of life. They forget what is really going on right outside their back door.

In-depth artist and writers look to nature for inspiration. Both Annie Dillard and Louise Erdrich look at nature and see that they would like to be animals. They think that to be an animal would be easier than a human. In "Skunk Dreams," Erdrich says, "If I were an animal, I'd choose a skunk: live fearlessly, eat anything, gestate my young in just two months, and fall into a state of dreaming torpor when the cold bit hard" (113). The skunks don't have to worry about growing up and how they are perceived and how they act. The skunk does not need to get upset or worry or feel insecure, and Erdrich, like every human in the world, is envious of a life like that. Erdrich is saying that she wants to live a simple life and not worry about things that she doesn't have to. Erdrich was only a teenager when she took her sleeping bag to the high school to camp the night away. Little did she know what kind of effect it would have on her. She says, "When I was fourteen, I slept alone on a North Dakota football field under cold stars on an early September night" (106). This was a time when Louise was starting high school, and her insecurities were beginning to appear. Erdrich took herself to the football field so that she could get away from everything, and just clear her mind, like many teenagers do at that age. Time to be alone and think is a wonderful thing for a teenager to have, and Erdrich did what she felt was right for her, to have peace and quiet and to be one with nature.

Annie Dillard describes how a weasel lives in her essay "Living Like Weasels." She says, "A weasel is wild. Who knows what he thinks? He sleeps in his underground den, his tail draped over his nose. Sometimes he lives in his den for two days without leaving" (656). Dillard is saying that weasels live a simple but intense life. They are able to eat, sleep, and live. Their only means of food and survival is their own keen wit and intuition. Dillard talks about how with one glance she was in a trance with a weasel. "I was stunned into stillness. . . . Our eyes locked, and someone threw away the key" (657). She goes on to describe the intensity of the weasel and how his glance was a "bright blow to the brain. . . . It felled the forest . . . and drained the pond" (657). Dillard is explaining how intense this weasel was and how she could never have had the same meeting with a human. Dillard thinks that humans are incapable of such feelings because we do not need to live with such intensity. To a weasel, meeting another animal or human in the woods means a potentially deadly encounter. So the weasel has a passion to stay alive and intimidate if it needs to. I imagine that people have feelings that can be compared to that of a weasel, but they rarely live up to them.

I have an Aunt Rosie who has experienced such intense feelings that in one moment her life changed forever. She tells the story of the first time she laid eyes on my uncle. She was sitting in a crowded cafe when all of a sudden the tall, dark, and skinny man of her dreams strolled into the crowded cafe and ordered a blueberry muffin. When he turned to find a seat, her eyes met his and locked. All they could focus on was each other. She says that it was as if the two of them were talking without words. Just looking in this stranger's eyes seemed to tell her all she needed to know about him. According to my aunt, at that moment nothing in the world mattered to her, not the man that was sitting next to her smoking in the non-smoking section, not even the couple two tables away who had just gotten engaged. To be so captivated in one person and not even know him—this is the closest feeling that I could compare with the animal magnetisms that the weasel has. Although there are special situations, usually we humans do not take notice of every thing around us like the weasel must. We just let people walk by us and think nothing of it.

Both authors are telling us that there is so much out there that people never realize or never get to experience, because they are too busy worrying with the things that keep them in their "cages." In particular people seem to stay in their own city "cages" because they feel safe and comfortable. They don't take chances, and they don't live life with the passion and intensity that animals do. Erdrich talks about the game preserve with the fence around it that could be torn down easily, but still the domesticated animals stay inside and do not venture out into the open wilderness. Erdrich talks about this fence that she walks along all of the time: "The walking lulls— . . . I ignore the fence. I walk along it as if it simply does not exist, as if I really am a part of that place just beyond my reach" (111). Erdrich is saying she does not even realize there is a barrier anymore, just like many people in the world today forget that they have other options.

Many people never leave the state that they live in, let alone the country, either because their lives are too busy or because they are afraid of what could happen to them while they are roaming free. Some of my best friends have never left the state of Pennsylvania. They find it completely amazing that I have lived in four other states. They gasp and say, "Wow, what is that like?" I just wonder why they haven't taken even a day trip somewhere they have never been, just to explore and see what there is to see. Traveling is a great way to experience something new and exciting. By not venturing into the great unknown, they are missing out on so much the world has to offer. I could not imagine staying in one place for my entire life. To me, it would make for a lackluster life.

My family and I make it a point to go somewhere every year, just to get away from everything and enjoy ourselves. This "see the world mentality" comes from my parents. When they were young, neither of them traveled much It was exactly an hour's drive to the beach for my mother and her family, which is the only place they ever got to go. My father's family never took vacations because with nine children leaving the fort was just too difficult. So now that my parents are older (when most people are starting to wind down), they seem to "kick things up a bit." They take every chance they get to break free and enjoy the world and nature around them; just a trip to the flower nursery is good enough for them. It is a great adventure. They can spend hours there just looking at all of the different kinds of flowers and plants that they have to choose from. My parents have even traveled to North Carolina from Pennsylvania to witness the azalea festival that is held there every year. It is nothing for my parents to pick up and take a nine hour drive just to load the van up full of flowers. It just shows how much they enjoy the combination of travel and nature.

A lot of people that we associate with create a nature of their own, to sort of make up for the nature that they don't get to experience in the outdoors. In my home, we have skylights that light up the house in the summer time and allow the sunlight to come to us when we just don't feel like being outside. My mother loves to have plants in the house; she takes care of them everyday and makes sure that she doesn't kill them. We have even raised a mini garden in our backyard. I guess it makes us feel close to nature. Along with the mini garden, we also have azaleas, sunflowers, shrubs and miniature trees that become transplanted into our front yard. There we can sit on our porch and get away from everything and enjoy the nature that my family has created. It is a space of our own.

Our little piece of land next to the street makes us feel miles away from anywhere. Like Dillard, who appears to be surrounded by nature at Hollins Pond but she is really standing just across the road from the highway, my family and I surround ourselves with nature so that we can try to forget the world that is around us for as long as we can. We say that we are "nature people" by having these things and enjoying the outdoors, but I think, like a lot of people, we are just fooling ourselves. We don't go hiking or camping like normal nature enthusiasts do, so it seems our nature is just a facade, but it seems to work for us.

Erdrich feels that people are moving too far away from where they should be, and I agree with her. We need to get back to living by necessity and not worrying about the little useless things in life. People are more worried about how many miles to the gallon their new car will get rather than about how many hours they will have to spend with their families. For many, life is just a daily, weekly, and yearly routine: Go to work, come home, play with our children, and then off to bed. It seems like an endless cycle until the man draped in black comes to take you away. This world has become too commercialized and people are taking nature and the world around them for granted. We need to start looking further than just our comfortable surroundings (our homes, yards, and cars) to find more in life. Then maybe we could enjoy ourselves and stop worrying so much.

Many people do not know how to change or will never take the time to change, and in continuing to be oblivious to the world around them, they are passing up the chance to experience life in all of its intensity. Maybe we need to sit back and look at the world for a minute and decide what is truly important and if money and material luxuries outweigh the family and natural luxuries. Both authors feel that people can do more with their lives and that we can learn a lot from animals and nature. If we take the time to listen to nature and understand all it has to offer, then maybe we can learn how to enjoy our lives and live in the moment, just as the skunk and weasel do.

Notes

1. What Is Personal Academic Writing?

1. Narrative theorists draw even more explicit distinctions. For example, in *Recent Theories of Narrative*, Wallace Martin explains that in autobiography, "someone describes the personal significance of past experiences from the perspective of the present." He distinguishes autobiography from

> the *memoir* (usually a record of events of public interest, such as a statesman's career), the *reminiscence* (a record of personal relationships and memories, without emphasis on the self), and the *journal* or *diary* (in which the immediate record of experience is not altered by later reflection). (75, emphasis added)

In his discussion of the essay genre, Douglas Hesse usefully outlines a continuum of narrative frameworks, distinguishing between stories *as* essays and essays *with* stories ("Stories in Essays"; "Essay Form"). In *Reading Autobiography: A Guide for Interpreting Life Narratives*, Sidonie Smith and Julia Watson provide a comprehensive account of the "fifty-two genres of life narrative." Tracing the roots of specific terms and alluding to relevant scholarship, their glossary (as well as their book) is an invaluable resource for researchers, teachers, and students of experiential writing.

For scholars of the essay, the *personal essay* does not necessarily include reference to the writer's experience. Although, as O. B. Hardison Jr. has remarked, trying to pin down the exact nature and form of the essay is "like trying to bind Proteus" (11), most theorists would agree that the personal essay incorporates observations about issues of life, whether social, political, or cultural, with observations gleaned from personal experience or introspection, although the actual experience may not be displayed or depicted in the text.

2. Dana C. Elder offers one of the best explanations of the personal essay that I've read: "Aesthetically pleasing, upon close analysis logically unified, rich in tropes, figures, and word play, the personal essay at its best combines in one seamless cloth the warp of poetics, the weave of rhetoric, and the colors of philosophy" (425). Elder's efforts are directed at moving students from essays of disclosure to "classical civic discourse forms which enfranchise the personal in the service of the community, thereby including both the expressive and the transactional" (426). She suggests that instead of personal narratives, students

be taught to write polemics, suasive essays, and paradoxical encomia.

3. Remarkably, as Lisa Ede pointed out at the 2002 Caucus on Intellectual Property and Composition/Communication Studies, citing Rebecca Moore Howard, the imperative to cite is inversely proportionate to a scholar's status in the field—for those who are best known, there is little need to prove that they have "done their homework."

4. For discussions of female ways of thinking, see germinal studies by, for example, Mary Belenky et al.; Nancy Chodorow; Elizabeth Flynn; and Carol Gilligan.

5. But Olivia Frey also asserts that "if it were not for women, we might not be questioning the way that we write literary criticism" (523). Richard Fulkerson provides a nice summary of recent feminist critiques of claims regarding women's cognitive and developmental inadequacies when it comes to constructing arguments (208–09).

6. Many feminist teachers and scholars in composition studies have embraced this critical stance, suggesting less adversarial alternatives for the teaching of writing. For example, Catherine E. Lamb recommends an instructional approach derived from mediation and negotiation theory, in which, like contemporary conflict resolution, the goal "is no longer to win but to arrive at a solution in a just way that is acceptable to both sides" (18). Sonja K. Foss and Cindy L. Griffin propose an "invitational argument," which encourages an internal process of transformation based on equality and respect for rhetor and audience members. For additional discussions of noncombative argument, see Andrea Lunsford and Lisa Ede; Dennis A. Lynch, Diana George, and Marilyn M. Cooper.

7. In his analysis of contemporary American literary nonfiction, Chris Anderson makes much the same point. Citing Kenneth Burke's *Rhetoric of Motives,* Anderson declares that all symbolic actions are rhetorically motivated: "At the root of every literary work and symbolic act is the 'invitation to purely formal assent. . . . Many purely formal patterns can readily awaken an attitude of collaborative expectancy in us' (58)" (*Style* 178). Argument, then, is not necessarily vindictive or agonistic; instead it can be an effort to construct meaning, based on the human "'rhetorical motive,' the instinct to engage in rhetorical exchange for the sake of the exchange itself" (Anderson, *Style* 178; Burke 136–37).

8. According to Susan Peck MacDonald, even the most stylistically controlled and impersonal academic writing reveals an epistemic component. Because scholars build knowledge as they compose, in part by acknowledging and developing previous scholarship, their texts center on collaboration. MacDonald examines "epistemic sentences" from recent composition research and finds that each does "crucial disciplinary work" that includes acknowledging others in the field, exposing different viewpoints, and revealing researchers' thinking

processes (120–23). MacDonald observes that such writing is not assaultive or self-promoting in the traditional sense; rather it contributes to "a cumulative body of knowledge suited to our goals as students of rhetoric" (123). Indeed, MacDonald worries that a shift toward personal, expressive writing powered by critiques of academic discourse may ultimately undermine gains in establishing composition's disciplinary credibility. Although I want to see personal evidence as a feature of academic discourse, I think that MacDonald and I share common concerns.

9. Calling into question positivist claims to the empirical authority, Linda Brodkey distinguishes between *interpretation* and *analysis* of ethnographic data and in doing so helps bring to center stage the ethnographer as interpreter and writer rather than ethnography as method. Reading ethnographic research, as well as research in other disciplines, as a rhetorical performance means that claims are recognized as "probable" positions, not statistical certainties. With this perspective, research outcomes are dependent more on conception, wherein researchers *construct* information by interpreting data, than on analysis, wherein researchers *discover* information in the data, which are then analyzed (Brodkey, "Writing Ethnographic" 27–31). Brodkey argues that while interpretive ethnographies are "more self-consciously narrated than traditional ethnographies," both approaches are equally important, for the "value of ethnography inheres . . . in the researcher's decision to examine lived cultural experience—to conceptualize it, reflect on it, narrate it, and evaluate it" (32) and thus to credit the experience of self and Other as evidence consistent with or opposed to both theoretical or statistical claims.

10. Although Richard McNabb's "Making the Gesture: Graduate Student Submissions and the Expectation of Journal Referees" makes a similar case, his example, a personal essay submitted to *Rhetoric Review,* is not without its problems. McNabb argues that grad students and junior colleagues who ignore or subvert established discourse conventions by way of personal voice or experience-based arguments will likely have their manuscripts rejected. However, according to editor Theresa Enos, all of the peer reviewers who received the essay in McNabb's example "replied similarly: the piece set up binaries too neatly—and violently and angrily—without offering readers an alternative" ("Gender" 67). Thus, while I believe that personal writing is still a privileged academic genre, I don't think that efforts to extend opportunities to disciplinary initiates should preclude the serious scrutiny and evaluation required for any scholarly work. In chapter 4, I discuss methods for evaluating experience-based discourse.

11. Ultimately, Karen Paley acknowledges,

> I too was "harsh" in my commentary on Faigley and Berlin . . . [but] I felt that either no response or a lighthearted one would not be useful in dispelling the perpetuation of an Other in our field that has be-

come serious enough to me to look like a kind of theoretical racism against one's colleagues. (192)

For me, Paley's victimization rhetoric is unsettling because it perpetuates a mindset that Debbie Mutnick characterizes as disciplinary schizophrenia (85). Mutnick attributes the "schism between process and social epistemic approaches" to "underlying issues of class and racial discrimination [that] have never been adequately addressed by either camp" (83). Like Paley, she sees expressive writing as an instrument for realizing social activist goals, but her observation about the conflicted theoretical positioning of our discipline is significant in itself.

12. In her study of gender and class constructions on television talk shows, Elizabeth Birmingham explains, "By presenting guests with whom the viewer wishes to be entirely unable to identify, talk shows are able to cast viewers in the role of voyeurs to reinforce viewers' feelings of superiority and belief in the system that has made them superior" (2). In our own discipline, Joseph Harris notes an increase in published interviews of well-known academics and suggests that our interest is "symptomatic of the fascination with celebrity that permeates our culture." "In the age of *People, Rikki Lake, and Lingua Franca*," Harris observes, "the personal does not always seem subversive" ("Person" 52).

13. For important discussions of the links between *pathos* and *catharsis*, see Jeffrey Walker; Dale L. Sullivan (115–16).

14. It should be emphasized that *catharsis* is an attribute of audiences, not of playwrights, and in the same way, the strategic use of *pathos*, the heightening of emotion by a speaker, is an audience-effect designed to elicit agreement in a rhetorical situation.

15. James L. Kinneavy defines *kairos* as "the right or opportune time to do something, or right measure in doing something" ("*Kairos*: A Neglected Concept" 80) and *prepon* as "the concept of fitness" or appropriateness ("*Kairos* in Aristotle's" 442). Discussing Paul Ricoeur, Michael Leff usefully explains rhetorical appropriateness or propriety in these terms: in judging the "requirements of proof relative to a specific group of auditors and a specific set of public circumstances," the ancients sought "decorum or propriety," understood as a "balance [in] the mode of expression against the occasion, the subject, and the interests of those who render judgment." Relatedly, he offers a contemporary understanding of argument: "This flexible, socially grounded, and audience-centered conception of argumentative proof demands that arguers exercise a form of balanced judgment." Leff shows that this kind of appropriate discourse is cognitive as well as stylistic (61).

16. In *Autobiographics*, Leigh Gillmore raises similar questions about the politics of confession as it relates to women's autobiographical narratives.

17. Narrowing the focus of this interrogation, Karen Surman Paley argues

that the family system is an essential site of character formation, intimately bound to an individual's political and ideological positionings. Hence, encouraging students to examine their family lives and values in relation to social questions about power and victimization can foster more (self) critical consciousness and contribute to significant social change (19–20). Further, in her ethnographic account of one student's critique of a government-sponsored program that placed inner-city children in suburban schools, a critique that moved from personal narrative to an exploration of racial issues, Paley reveals a process wherein "classrooms open to personal writing can produce essays that have significance outside the classroom" (160).

18. For a detailed account of the postmodern critique of the subject, see Paul Smith.

19. Joan W. Scott cites Michel de Certeau, "The place where discourse is produced is relevant" (qtd. in Scott, "Evidence" 789), to stress the importance of understanding the ways experiences have been configured for the narrator of any historical account and to point out how often "power and politics in these [traditional] notions of knowledge and experience" remain hidden or obscured ("Evidence" 783; see also Bérubé 1065).

2. The Personal Is Rhetorical

1. In "Notes on a Politics of Location," Rich seems wary of theory, which she defines as the antithesis of material, physical particularity. She writes,

> Begin with the material. Pick up the long struggle against lofty and privileged abstraction. . . . Theory—the seeing of patterns, showing the forest as well as the trees—theory can be a dew that rises from the earth and collects in a rain cloud and returns to earth over and over. But if it doesn't smell of the earth, it isn't good for the earth. (213–14)

Rather than rejecting theory, Kirsch and Ritchie show that we can use Rich's "politics of location" to interrogate theory and the practices that support it.

2. In his comprehensive analysis of contemporary subjectivity, Paul Smith explains these etymological distinctions:

> The "individual" is that which is undivided and whole, and understood to be the source and agent of conscious action or meaning which is consistent with it. The "subject," on the other hand, is not self-contained, as it were, but is immediately cast into a conflict with forces that dominate it in some way or another—social formations, language, political apparatuses, and so on. The "subject," then, is determined—the object of determinant forces; whereas "the individual" is assumed to be determining. (xxxiii–xxxiv)

3. Enlisting Gayatri Spivak's concept of the "double session," Susan Jarratt describes feminist rhetoric as

> simultaneously naming and reconstructing difference. In other words, rhetoric understood as a dual process of representation—as both a figurative and political act—gives names to language that articulates difference while exposing the power relations at work in acts of naming. To apply this idea to women as a group is to see women not as a natural class but as a group with shifting boundaries, capable of being constituted in any historical moment or context through the symbolic and political acts of those in the group and those outside it. ("Introduction" 9)

4. One example of this approach is Pamela L. Caughie's essay, "Let It Pass: Changing the Subject, Once Again," which invokes the concept of racial "passing" as a way of understanding and interrogating subject positions, rather than envisioning and assuming a singular female identity or representation.

5. David Bartholomae states in his "Reply to Stephen North,"

> It is wrong to teach late-adolescents that writing is an expression of individual thoughts and feelings. It makes them suckers and, I think, it makes them powerless, at least to the degree that it makes them blind to tradition, power, and authority as they are present in language and culture. (128–29)

Bartholomae's response here and elsewhere is part of a broader debate about the usefulness and value of encouraging students to write personal, rather than academic, discourse.

6. In large part, this kind of misreading has been promoted by essayists themselves, who, starting with Montaigne, have insisted that the self on the page is synonymous with the writing self (Klaus, "Montaigne," "Essayists"). Moreover, in her analysis of fictive narration, Susan Sniader Lanser notes that unless a text is "marked" to the contrary, readers will typically equate the voice, vision, ideology, and, perhaps, the narrative style of narrator with those same attributes of the textual author (150–53; see also Chatman, *Story* 151).

7. In this regard, Miecke Bal states that characteristics of an implied author are determined retrospectively by the reader, whereas the narrator contributes to the text's developing meaning (120). In later writing, Booth called more attention to effects of culture and literature on writers and audiences, as well as to the implied values and beliefs of writers and potential readers evoked textually. These considerations both undercut and clarified his initial rigid distinctions (415, 421–23).

8. Among current theorists, there is some agreement that within the fa-

miliar space of the *polis,* the reputation and character of the citizen-speaker were already known to the audience (Ronald). Moreover, Nan Johnson sees inevitable coherence between the classical speaker's actual character and his or her discursive self-portrayal, since, she argues, Aristotelian ethos means "investing [various kinds of speeches] with moral character[, which] requires that the orator understand human nature and emotions—in short, that he understand the Good in a variety of situations" (101). In her view, the *Rhetoric* was an effort to train young orators to practice the Good by engaging in "any activity that follows a rational principle" and to develop moral virtue as "the ability to choose conduct in accordance with moral custom" (102). Certainly in the case of Grobman, whose scholarly essay serves as my first example, the narrator's rhetorical ethos matches the moral convictions of the writer.

Furthermore, the concepts of *ethos* and *persona* seem to merge for nonfiction texts although, technically, there are distinctions between them. For Roger Cherry, the difference between the two concepts is particularly crucial. As he sees it, in "nonliterary" discourse, ethos is achieved when the writer's biographical (that is confirmable) facts and intellectual competence are revealed through the text, while the roles that the narrator assumes and the personality that is projected are part and parcel of the narrator's *persona.* In the discussion of scientific models, ethos is seen as a representation of the author's genuine knowledge of his subject, scholarly integrity, and awareness of audience needs. Persona is essentially the tone of voice and character represented by the style, diction, and mood of the text. Cherry's view of ethos in nonfiction writing suggests the importance of using personal reference and personal experience to inspire confidence by portraying the writer's professionalism and expertise. Other commentators more closely link ethos and persona. For Theresa Enos, for example, both ethos and *persona,* a term she uses interchangeably with *voice,* emerge from the rhetorical category of delivery. In Enos's terms, *style* refers to thought, words, and voice, presented or delivered to the audience to solicit identification. Ethos emerges as a product of voice; we believe the voice, identify with it, trust it as "character." In writing, she says, the verbal patterns are consciously selected to project an ethos ("Voice" 186). Because voice is dialogic, it cannot be created in a vacuum and must always engage an audience's participation and ultimately its identification.

9. Using Plato's *Phaedrus* as her point of departure, Susan Wells argues that rhetorical discourse is always "a doubled performance." By this she means that implied in the rhetorical act is a *"fictional* position of stability," which appears "as something provisional and temporary, rather than as the truth of the speaker or of the genre" ("Doubleness" 119–20). Awareness of the fictivity of the rhetorical subject or "permission to lie," Wells says, "is one of the most valuable gifts that a teacher can give to students" (119).

10. For a nice explanation of distinctions between Bakhtin's concept of double-voicedness in novels versus double-voicedness in rhetoric, see Wells ("Doubleness" 120–21).

11. Kamler develops her transformational theory from her reading of G. Kress's social semiotic theory of representation and from a notion of design advanced by Kress in association with the New London Group (51–54.)

12. Although distinctions between essays and academic articles endure (e.g., Zeiger; W. Harris; Bloom, "Essay"; Atkins; Spellmeyer; Core), my colleagues generally speak of both "scholarly essays" and "scholarly articles" as one and the same, regardless of their inclusion of personal accounts or disclosures, as do many prestigious journals (e.g., the PMLA's statement of editorial policy continues to solicit *essays* for publication, although CCC asks for *articles*). Because I want to argue for further blurring of generic conventions, I use the term *essay* for both types of writing.

13. The overarching structure of Alice Walker's "Beyond the Peacock: The Reconstruction of Flannery O'Connor" might be described as coming close to Douglas Hesse's definition of a horizontal narrative. In this form, the essay seems "to exist because of the story" and "the discursive elements of such pieces function to develop their stories more than the stories function to clarify some point" ("Essay Form" 300). Hesse asserts that stories in narrative essays persuade in part because they formalize experience into acceptable patterns that we are conditioned to accept and in part because, being grounded in a particular place and time, they are relieved of the burden of proof ("Stories"). Thus Hesse would say that the events as well as the exposition in Walker's essay are internally propositional but ultimately do not provide proof or evidence in the same way that traditional arguments do. Of course, "Beyond the Peacocks" is not a thesis-proof essay, but all the same, Walker does *prove* a number of points, invoking as evidentiary her own lived experiences and her experiences of "reading" O'Connor. Ultimately, she proves that if we are going to get at the wholeness of history or the wholeness of literature, it will be contradictory and misshapen; she proves too that such efforts will inspire anger and grief and reconciliation without forgiving or forgetting.

14. Burke states, "For substance, in the old philosophies, was an *act;* and a way of life is an *acting-together;* and in acting together, men [humans] have common sensations, concepts, images, ideas, attitudes that make then *consubstantial*" (*Rhetoric* 21, emphasis in original). According to Dale L. Sullivan, in addition to providing good reasons, classical speakers generated this sense of consubstantiality "by engaging the audience in a conversation that transcends time," bringing speaker and audience together into a common space (126).

15. In his discussion of Joan Didion, Chris Anderson demonstrates that specific, elaborated detail can work to deny abstraction, forcing the reader to

accept moral responsibility for the events depicted. Anderson argues that in Didion's essays

> abstractions are immoral because they are too easy and because they cover up. The particular requires discipline, a mastery of complexity, a sympathy for fact, a capacity for layered and nuanced interpretation, for tentativeness, openendedness, honesty. (*Style* 166)

16. Not coincidentally, Walker describes the ability to invoke both similarity and difference as "a kind of grace" in Flannery O'Connor's maturing fiction. She explains,

> She retained a certain distance . . . from the inner workings of her black characters. . . . [B]y deliberately limiting her treatment of them to cover their observable demeanor and actions, she leaves them free, in the reader's imagination, to inhabit another landscape, another life, than the one she creates for them. (52)

By pronouncing difference, O'Connor drew her African American characters more as living people and less as stock characters or stereotypes.

17. Walker's ambiguous rendering of her mother reminds me of Grace Paley's introductory comment in *Enormous Changes at the Last Minute:* "Everyone in this book is imagined into life except the father. No matter what story he has to live in, he's my father, I. Goodside, M.D., artist and storyteller" (iv).

3. Constructing Experience

1. Following Hayden White's understanding of historical narrativity, Cheryl Glenn asserts that "all historical accounts, even the most seemingly objective historical records, are stories. And even these stories are selected and arranged according to the selector's frame of reference" (388). Glenn observes that most historiographers share this postmodern methodological perspective; they "already take for granted that histories . . . fulfill our needs at a particular time and place, and that they never and have never reflected a neutral reality" (388).

2. Jacques Derrida uses the dual concepts of "differance" (to name, first, the relative *differences* that make meaning meaningful and, second, the indefinitely prolonged deferral of any "ultimate" meaning) and "trace" to argue that we cannot return to a point of origin or make our experiences "present" in thought, memory, or writing. All we have are signs or representations of "intuitive experience," never the "'thing itself'" (see, especially, 60–62).

3. The seminal research projects of Belenky et al. and Nancy Chodorow, among others, drew attention to the ways in which our reading of experience

is anticipated by the social categories through which our sense of identity is constructed.

4. In Joan W. Scott's view, redefining and analyzing experience as a concept "entails focusing on processes of identity production, insisting on the discursive nature of 'experience' and on the politics of its construction" ("Evidence" 797).

5. According to Susan Wells, rhetorical texts always encompass a fictive element because they are from the start "double-voiced" constructions. As such,

> the double-voiced rhetorical text does not locate itself on the sublime terrain of historical inevitability. . . . The multivoiced text permits the writer's location in time to be deployed and activated within the text, to become an element in the persuasive project or in the work of exposition. ("Doubleness" 120–21)

6. Philippe Lejeune coined the term *autobiographical pact* to describe the autobiographer's willingness and ability to recount events as they "actually" happened and to convey them to the reader. According to Paul John Eakin,

> [m]ost critics today would concur with Lejeune's enlightened view of the nature of autobiographical truth, which recognizes that autobiography is necessarily in its deepest sense a special kind of fiction, its self and its truth as much created as (re)discovered realities. In this matter of reference and truth, however, Lejeune's own posture with regard to autobiographical practice is instructively ambivalent. (*Touching* 25)

7. Recognizing the sociocultural role of identity construction in the interpretation of experience, Eakin cautions against reading autobiographical accounts as exclusive representations of autonomous subjectivity, on the one hand, or cultural and linguistic determinism, on the other. "It is surely no accident," Eakin states,

> that autobiography and its sustaining myth of the autonomous self have become a preferred mode of expression for the oppressed in our time. . . . Autobiography, however, is by its very nature a distinctly ambiguous mode of self-assertion, for the self is shaped by culture every bit as much in its writing as in its living. (*Touching* 88)

Eakin thus describes the self of autobiography as "doubly structured, doubly mediated," explaining that "the self is already constructed in interaction with others of its culture before it begins self-consciously in maturity (and specifically in autobiography—where it exists) to think in terms of models of identity." Eakin names this textually inscribed autobiographical self "a construct of construct" (*Touching* 102).

8. Students' memoirs and personal narratives reveal most vividly their reconstructions and fictionalizations of lived experience. Obviously, students will use similar strategies in other kinds of writing, but their adaptations tend to be more difficult to discern and less likely to be the focus of student-and-teacher dialogue. I have selected my examples from personal narratives because they so clearly illustrate students' stratagems at work.

9. Judith Summerfield theorizes responses like mine to students' recon-structive renderings by asking

> if we need to know, or should even inquire, whether there is a life in the text, whether students are telling the "truth." Is it any of our business? If we do inquire, aren't we ourselves conflating the life and the text? Shouldn't our business be language, an exploration with our students about the writerly choices of, say, narrating? (188)

10. Of particular interest in this regard is Eakin's analysis of autobiogra-phy and reference in *Roland Barthes by Roland Barthes* (*Touching* 15–23).

11. Despite their careful attention to context, feminist historians can find themselves in what looks like a no-win situation, as revealed in Xin Lu Gale's recent critique of studies about Aspasia of Miletus written by Cheryl Glenn and by Susan Jarratt and Rory Ong. Gale attacks feminist methodologies that in-volve interpretation, suggesting that such approaches may privilege feminist agendas at the expense of traditional philological methods and primary tex-tual evidence. In her response to Gale's essay, Glenn emphasizes the "fruitful and necessary tension between history and history writing" (388) and explains that "postmodern historiography does not attempt to do away with the notion of truth; instead, it attempts to think of truth outside the confines of mythical objectivity, or, at the very least, to decouple the link between 'objectivity' and 'truth'" (387).

12. Accepting that relations between the researcher and her research are incontrovertibly enmeshed, anthropologist Ruth Behar makes the practice cen-tral to her collection of ethnographic essays. Behar uses the term *vulnerable* to capture the personal stake involved when the field research comes to "a keen understanding of what aspects of the self are the most important filters through which one perceives the world and, more particularly, the topic being studied" (13). In *The Vulnerable Observer: Anthropology That Breaks Your Heart,* the eth-nographer's "location" (emotionally, socially, culturally, and so on) is folded into the ethnographic method, and the ethnographer's history and experiences be-come data for the project. Behar admits her complicity in her ethnographic con-struction, admits that her private fears and concerns are the lens through which she reports her findings. Paralleling her investigation of the agricultural com-munity of Santa Maria del Monte in northern Spain, and serving as a backdrop to her fieldwork, is the impending and subsequent death of her grandfather.

The anthropologist's guilt at leaving the United States at this critical moment self-consciously colors her observations and conclusions. Because Behar first foregrounds her emotional conflicts, she feels free to acknowledge the interpretiveness of her richly textured interviews with mothers and grown daughters, with older farmers who have lost wives and companions, and with the village priest. Despite the problems associated with such blurrings, accusations of sentimentality, of appropriative identification rather than difference, Behar argues that invocations to the researcher's experience enhance ethnographic analysis by enlarging as well as limiting the "picture" under investigation.

13. Narrative theorists use the term *narratee* to describe the reader's role in these instances.

14. In addition to personal reference and direct address, Yancey subverts traditional academic discourse by using a variety of discursive patterns and styles of writing as well as typographical variations.

4. Valuing Personal Evidence

1. The *Rhetoric* is inconsistent in its treatment of pathos and ethos in terms of how these forms of appeal are related to logos. In Book 1 and at times in Book 3, both are viewed as lesser strategies, lacking the status of logical demonstrations, and something to be avoided. Yet in Book 2, Aristotle not only gives them equal standing but provides extensive advice about their uses in successive arguments. However, the case has been made repeatedly that Book 2 was a later addition and that it was inserted randomly, without efforts to accommodate its assertions to those expressed in the other books.

2. Ronald states that her essay responds to Robert Connors and S. Michael Halloran, who argue in separate articles that classical rhetoric was entirely a public discourse.

3. Of course, arguments by means of narrative go back at least to the Sophists, and claims to personal experience are found in notable orations and writings as early as the time of Seneca. Consider Gorgias's "story" of Helen, a narrative argument deriving from and invoking narrative. Plato too uses stories throughout his dialogues, both as illustrative paradigms and as supplements to the central argument.

4. Although Douglas Hesse focuses on personal essays, his theory of narrative proof is relevant. According to this view, stories in essays don't prove points in the customary sense; rather they create a place within the text for the proposition to occur. Because the proposition has an apparently appropriate relationship to the story that accompanies it, the reader accepts the proposition's validity. The evidence provided by the story is not "sufficient;" rather it is "associative." Readers come to be persuaded as they are "moving . . . through narrative from one scene to another" ("Stories" 187–88), and because they are

familiar with and readily receptive to stories, they are willing to accept propositions put forth within the narrative's limits. Further, in contrast to other kinds of arguments whose proofs are represented as "timeless, logical, and stable," Hesse says, the "truth" of essays is always understood to be "situational, constructed in experience" and thus always contingent ("Experience" 199).

5. In *Rhetoric* and in *Prior Analytics, example* is defined as rhetorical induction; like its counterpart in formal logic or dialectic, it implies that a generalization will be gathered from the presentation of particulars, although with example the generalization is often applied to additional cases or situations.

6. Following a similar line of analysis, John T. Gage observes that "the enthymeme cannot be constructed in the absence of a dialectical relation with an audience, since it is only through what the audience contributes that the enthymeme exists as such" (157), and further that "Aristotle discusses the unsaid parts of a narrative and of a metaphor in the same way in which he discusses the unsaid parts of an enthymeme, as that which is supplied by the hearer" (282, n. 14). Underscoring the logical reasoning required for the construction of Aristotelian examples as arguments, William Grimaldi states that "in using an example some transition to the universal has already been made by the mind if the mind is to discern any likeness or relevance of the example in the first place" (105; qtd. in Benoit 185). Notably, within the rhetorical maneuvers of induction are opportunities for the audience to participate in the act of argument formation. Thus readers do not passively accept examples or stories, personal or otherwise. They are always already weighing, evaluating, applying, or rejecting evidence on the basis of its logical cogency.

7. For debates on the logical construction of Aristotle's examples, see Grimaldi; Benoit; Hauser.

8. Burke argues that it can be worthwhile to build "a *terministic* bridge whereby one realm is *transcended* by being viewed *in terms of* a realm 'beyond' it'" ("I" 877, emphasis in original). As Burke explains it, transcendence is a symbolic movement toward a new perspective, a redescription: "And insofar as things here and now are treated in terms of a 'beyond,' they thereby become infused or inspirited by the addition of a *new* or *further dimension*" ("I" 880, emphasis in original). By bridging experiential and academic discourses, for example, writers and readers can reach toward a further, or alternative, orientation and thus toward a more complicated description of the world. The need for overlapping worldviews or orientations as integral to promoting human understanding is further defined up by Burkean critic Angus Fletcher. Invoking a racing metaphor, Fletcher explains that in the moment when the baton is handed from one runner to the next, there is for a brief time a kind of overlap or bridging, as the two runners move forward together. Fletcher argues that Burke

> has specified the necessity of overlap, if we are to continue to communicate without dropping the age-old baton of the cry for "more

humanity," not less. More handing on, not less. . . . None of us can reach the ultimate shore. Only the sense that enough love and enough knowledge move us to reach out toward it, beyond our hidden selves, can constitute our small portion of success. (172)

9. In addition to Fisher, other notable theorists who have argued for narration as a central mode of human communication and understanding include M. M. Bakhtin, Jean-François Lyotard, and Fredric Jameson. Also similar to Fisher's worldview paradigms is Jerome Bruner's examination of ways of knowing. Bruner distinguishes between the narrative and logo-scientific modes, privileging, like Fisher, the narrative mode for its shifting possibilities, uncertainties, and contradictions. Where Fisher embeds rational understanding within narrative understanding, Bruner keeps the modes separate and distinct.

10. Harpham's essay aims at developing a theory of ethical reasoning, which takes into consideration the ethical implications of literature. What has relevance here is his understanding of the "play" between narrative and theory.

11. We in composition face much the same problem of evidence that Joan W. Scott describes for historians:

> When the evidence offered is the evidence of "experience," the claim for referentiality is further buttressed—what could be truer, after all, than a subject's own account of what he or she lived through? It is precisely this kind of appeal to experience as incontestable evidence and as an originary point of explanation—as a foundation on which analysis is based—that weakens the critical thrust of histories of difference. ("Evidence" 777)

Scott's main point is that appeals to experience are reductive and aligned with an identity politics that closes down the possibilities of conversations across constructed social categories:

> Questions about the constructed nature of experience, about how subjects are constituted as different in the first place, about how one's vision is structured—about language (or discourse) and history— are left aside. The evidence of experience then becomes evidence for the fact of difference, rather than a way of exploring how difference is established, how it operates, how and in what ways it constitutes subjects who see and act in the world. ("Evidence 777)

12. Emphasizing the contradictions, allegiances, and challenges of contemporary notions of evidence, Heather Dubrow reminds us that historically for western European cultures, *evidence* was understood as something "out there," hard cold facts waiting to be discovered and named as evidentiary. Today, however, we recognize the rhetoricalness of evidence and evidentiary

procedures and, as a result, at least in some circles (Dubrow identifies the Foucaultian anecdote of new historicism), research seems to favor "singularity" rather than "reduplication" (13). Of particular concern to Dubrow, then, is the potential erosion of academic rigor caused by an emphasis on performance, especially the way an argument is made to appear "provocative" or "interesting," instead of evidential (16).

13. For critiques and extensions of Fisher's values approach to narrative, see Lucaites and Condit; Farrell; McGee and Nelson; Bennett and Edelman; Rowland.

14. Similar criteria are used to evaluate postmodern and feminist histories, Susan Jarratt explains. Critics ask such questions as "Does this history instruct, delight, and move the reader? Is the historical data probable? Does it fit with other accounts or provide a convincing alternative?" ("Comment" 391).

5. Teaching Personal Academic Argument

1. In this chapter, I discuss a number of anthologized essays and articles that appear in the assignment samples and to which students refer in their essays. The following essays and articles were assigned readings and the bases of writing assignments during different semesters. From Donald McQuade and Robert Atwan, eds., *The Writer's Presence: A Pool of Readings,* 3rd ed.: Russell Baker, "Gumption" (62–68); Raymond Carver, "My Father's Life" (69–75); Judith Cofer, "Silent Dancing" (76–84); John Grisham, "Unnatural Killers" (691–99); Jamaica Kinkaid, "Biography of a Dress" (130–37); Gary Soto, "The Childhood Worries, or Why I Became a Writer" (255–64); Alice Walker, "Beauty: When the Other Dancer Is the Self" (285–91); Eudora Welty, "The Little Store" (600–06); Marie Winn, "TV Addiction" (607–09). From Marjorie Ford, Jon Ford, and Ann Watters, eds., *Coming from Home: Readings for Writers:* David Elkind, "The Child Inside" (328–35); Susan Newby Short, "The Whispering of the Walls" (81–86); Tillie Olsen, "I Stand Here Ironing" (366–72); Elizabeth Stone, "Family Myths: Explanation Myths" (147–50); Judith Wallerstein and Sandra Blakeslee, "On the Brow of the Hill" (343–54); Marie Winn, "Television and Family Rituals" (174–82).

2. I acknowledge the very real danger of responding to personal narratives without interrogating their assumptions. To emphasize that the teacher's instructional role must always move beyond reactions to the formal attributes of the writing, Barbara Kamler presents two student papers, a child's "recipe" for turning girls into concrete and a college-level essay on marital servitude. Likewise, Richard E. Miller, citing Scott Lankford, illustrates the problems involved in responding to criminal and homophobic disclosures.

3. Carla's narrative replays a traditional tale of a woman's role in keeping home and hearth intact. Regardless of our knowledge of Carla's text as *fic-*

tion, following Kamler's suggestion, Carla's classmates and I might have learned a great deal by regarding her text as *representation.* We might have explored her investment in telling the story in this particular way; we might have interrogated her decision to represent this particular fiction as opposed to others. In such acts of reader and writer analysis, Kamler says, we learn to "relocate the personal in [its] larger social and political contexts" (183).

4. I am grateful to Bruce Ballenger for suggesting this type of exercise and for pointing out the usefulness of Tompkins's essay.

Works Cited

Addison, Joanne, and Sharon James McGee, eds. "Introduction." *Feminist Empirical Research: Emerging Perspectives on Qualitative and Teacher Research*. Portsmouth: Boynton/Cook, 1999. 1–7.

Anderson, Chris, ed. *Literary Nonfiction: Theory, Criticism, Pedagogy*. Carbondale: Southern Illinois UP, 1989.

———. *Style as Argument: Contemporary American Nonfiction*. Carbondale: Southern Illinois UP, 1987.

Anderson, Rebecca S., and Bruce W. Speck. "Suggestions for Responding to the Dilemma of Grading Students' Writing." *English Journal* 86 (1997): 21–27.

Anson, Chris M. "Introduction: Response to Writing and the Paradox of Uncertainty." Anson, *Writing* 1–11.

———, ed. *Writing and Response: Theory, Practice, and Research*. Urbana: NCTE, 1989.

Aristotle. *Nicomachean Ethics*. Trans. with introd. and notes by Terence Irwin. Indianapolis: Hackett, 1985.

———. *On Rhetoric: A Theory of Civic Discourse*. Trans. with introd., notes, and apps. by George A. Kennedy. New York: Oxford UP, 1991.

———. *Prior Analytics*. Trans. A. J. Jenkinson. *The Basic Works of Aristotle*. Ed. Richard McKeon. New York: Random, 1941. 62–107.

Atkins, G. Douglas. "Envisioning the Stranger's Heart." *College English* 56 (1994): 629–41.

Bakhtin, M. M. "Discourse in the Novel." *The Dialogic Imagination*. Trans. Caryl Emerson and Michael Holquist. Ed. Michael Holquist. Austin: U of Texas P, 1981.

Bal, Miecke. *Narratology: Introduction to the Theory of the Narrative*. Trans. Christine Van Boheemen. Toronto: U of Toronto P, 1985.

Ballenger, Bruce. E-mail to the author. 12 Dec. 2002.

Baradine, Bryan A., Molly Schmitz Baradine, and Elizabeth F. Deegan. "Beyond the Red Pen: Clarifying Our Role in the Response Process." *English Journal* 90 (2000): 94–101.

Barthes, Roland. *Roland Barthes by Roland Barthes*. Trans. Richard Howard. New York: Farrar, 1977.

Bartholomae, David. "A Reply to Stephen North." *PRE/TEXT* 11 (Spring-Summer 1990): 121–30.

———. "Writing with Teachers: A Conversation with Peter Elbow." *CCC* 46 (1995): 62–71.

Bazerman, Charles. "The Writing of Scientific Non-Fiction." *PRE/TEXT* 5 (1984): 39–74.

Behar, Ruth. *The Vulnerable Observer: Anthropology That Breaks Your Heart.* Boston: Beacon, 1996.

Belenky, Mary Field, Blythe McVicker Clinchy, Nancy Rule Goldberger, and Jill Mattuck Tarule. *Women's Ways of Knowing: The Development of Self, Voice, and Mind.* New York: Basic, 1986.

Benoit, William Lyon. "Aristotle's Example: The Rhetorical Induction." *Quarterly Journal of Speech* 66 (1980): 182–92.

Bennett, W. Lance, and Murray J. Edelman. "Toward a New Political Narrative." *Journal of Communication* 35 (1985): 156–71.

Berlin, James. "Rhetoric and Ideology in the Writing Class." *College English* 50 (1988): 477–94.

———. *Rhetoric and Reality: Writing Instruction in American Colleges, 1900–1985.* Carbondale: Southern Illinois UP, 1987.

Bérubé, Michael. "Against Subjectivity." *PMLA* 111 (Oct. 1996): 1063–68.

Birmingham, Elizabeth. "Fearing the Freak: How Talk TV Articulates Women and Class." *Journal of Popular Film and Television* 28 (Fall 2000): 133–39.

Bishop, Wendy. "I-Witnessing in Composition: Turning Ethnographic Data into Narratives." *Rhetoric Review* 11 (1992): 147–58.

———. "Students' Stories and the Variable Gaze of Composition Research." *Writing Ourselves into the Story: Unheard Voices from Composition Studies.* Ed. Sheryl I. Fontaine and Susan Hunter. Carbondale: Southern Illinois UP, 1993. 197–214.

———. "Suddenly Sexy: Creative Nonfiction Rear-ends Composition." *College English* 65 (2003): 257–75.

Bizzell, Patricia. "Cognition, Convention, and Certainty: What We Need to Know about Writing." *PRE/TEXT* 3 (1982): 213–43. Rpt. in *Cross-Talk in Comp Theory: A Reader.* Ed. Victor Villanueva Jr. Urbana: NCTE, 1997. 365–89.

———. "College Composition: Initiation into the Academic Discourse Community." *Curriculum Inquiry* 12 (1982): 191–207.

———. "Hybrid Academic Discourses: What, Why, How." *Composition Studies* 27 (Fall 1999): 7–21.

Bleich, David. "Reconceiving Literacy: Language Use and Social Relations." Anson, *Writing* 15–36.

Bloom, Lynn Z. "The Essay Canon." *College English* 61 (1999): 401–30.

———. "Living to Tell the Tale: The Complicated Ethics of Creative Nonfiction." *College English* 65 (2003): 276–89.

———. "Teaching College English as a Woman." *College English* 54 (1992): 818–25.

———. Why Don't We Write What We Teach? And Publish It? *JAC* 10 (1990): 87–100.

Bolker, Joan. "Teaching Griselda to Write." *College English* 40 (1979): 906–08.

Boone, Joseph A. Comment in "Forum: The Inevitability of the Personal." *PMLA* 111 (Oct. 1996): 1152–54.

Booth, Wayne C. *The Rhetoric of Fiction.* 2nd ed. Chicago: U of Chicago P, 1983.

Brady, Laura. "The Reproduction of Othering." Jarratt and Worsham 21–44.

Brannon, Lil, and C. H. Knoblauch. "On Students' Rights to Their Own Texts: A Model of Teacher Response." *CCC* 33 (1982): 157–66.

Bridwell-Bowles, Lillian. "Freedom, Form, Function: Varieties of Academic Discourse." *CCC* 46 (1995): 46–61.

Brodkey, Linda. "Writing Ethnographic Narratives." *Written Communication* 4 (1987): 25–50.

———. "Writing on the Bias." *College English* 56 (1994): 527–47.

Bruffee, Kenneth A. *Collaborative Learning: Higher Education, Interdependence, and the Authority of Knowledge.* Baltimore: Johns Hopkins UP, 1993.

Bruner, Jerome S. *Actual Minds, Possible Worlds.* Cambridge: Harvard UP, 1986.

Burke, Kenneth. "I, Eye, Ay—Emerson's Early Essay on 'Nature': Thoughts on the Machinery of Transcendence." *Sewanee Review* 74 (1966): 875–95.

———. *Permanence and Change: An Anatomy of Purpose.* 3rd ed. Berkeley: U of California P, 1984.

———. *A Rhetoric of Motives.* Berkeley: U of California P, 1969.

Butrym, Alexander J., ed. *Essays on the Essay: Redefining the Genre.* Athens: U of Georgia P, 1989.

Carver, Raymond. "Creative Writing 101." *The Story and Its Writer.* 5th ed. Ed. Ann Charters. Boston: Bedford/St. Martin's, 1999. 1583–86.

Caughie, Pamela L. "Let It Pass: Changing the Subject, Once Again." Jarratt and Worsham 111–31.

Chatman, Seymour. *Coming to Terms: The Rhetoric of Narrative in Fiction and Film.* Ithaca: Cornell UP, 1990.

———. *Story and Discourse: Narrative Structure in Film and Fiction.* Ithaca: Cornell UP, 1978.

Cherry, Roger D. "*Ethos* Versus Persona: Self-Representation in Written Discourse." *Written Communication* 5 (1988): 251–76.

Chodorow, Nancy. *The Reproduction of Mothering: Psychoanalysis and the Sociology of Gender.* Berkeley: U of California P, 1978.

Clark, Suzanne. "Argument and Composition." Jarratt and Worsham 94–99.

———. "Rhetoric, Social Construction, and Gender: Is It Bad to Be Sentimental?" Clifford and Schilb 96–108.

Clifford, John. "The Subject in Discourse." *Contending with Words: Composition and Rhetoric in a Postmodern Age.* Ed. Patricia Harkin and John Schilb. New York: MLA, 1991. 38–51.

Clifford, John, and John Schilb, eds. *Writing Theory and Critical Theory.* New York: MLA, 1994.

Connors, Robert. "Personal Writing Assignments." *CCC* 38 (1987): 166–83.

Connors, Robert J., Lisa S. Ede, and Andrea A. Lunsford, eds. *Essays on Classical Rhetoric and Modern Discourse*. Carbondale: Southern Illinois UP, 1984.

Core, George. "Stretching the Limits of the Essay." Butrym 207–20.

Couser, G. Thomas. *Altered Egos: Authority in American Autobiography*. New York: Oxford UP, 1989.

Daiker, Donald. "Learning to Praise." Anson, *Writing* 103–13.

Davidson, Cathy N. "Critical Fictions." *PMLA* 111 (Oct. 1996): 1069–71.

Deans, Thomas. *Writing Partnerships: Service-Learning in Composition*. Urbana: NCTE, 2000.

Derrida, Jacques. *Of Grammatology*. Trans. Gayatri Chakravorty Spivak. Baltimore: Johns Hopkins UP, 1976.

Dillard, Annie. "Living Like Weasels." McQuade and Atwan 655–59. Rpt. from *Teaching a Stone to Talk*. New York: Harper, 1982.

Dubrow, Heather. "The Status of Evidence." *PMLA* 111 (Jan. 1996): 7–20.

Eakin, Paul John. *Fictions in Autobiography: Studies in the Art of Self-Invention*. Princeton: Princeton UP, 1985.

———. *Touching the World: Reference in Autobiography*. Princeton: Princeton UP, 1992.

Elbow, Peter. "Reflections on Academic Discourse: How It Relates to Freshmen and Colleagues." *College English* 53 (1991): 135–55.

———. *Writing Without Teachers*. 2nd ed. New York: Oxford UP, 1998.

Elder, Dana C. "Expanding the Scope of Personal Writing in the Composition Classroom." *Teaching English in the Two-Year College TETYC* 27 (2000): 425–33.

Elkind, David. "The Child Inside." *Coming from Home: Readings for Writers*. Ed. Ford, Ford, and Watters. New York: McGraw, 1993. 328–35.

Enos, Theresa. "Gender and Publishing Scholarship in Rhetoric and Composition." Olson and Taylor 57–72.

———. "Voice as Echo of Delivery, *Ethos* as Transforming Process." *Composition in Context: Essays in Honor of Donald C. Stewart*. Ed. W. Ross Winterowd and Vincent Gillespie. Carbondale: Southern Illinois UP, 1992. 180–95.

Erdrich, Louise. "Skunk Dreams." McQuade and Atwan 106–13. Rpt. from *The Blue Jay's Dance*. New York: Harper, 1995.

Faigley, Lester. "Judging Writing, Judging Selves." *CCC* 40 (1989): 395–412.

Farrell, Thomas B. "Narrative in Natural Discourse: On Conversation and Rhetoric." *Journal of Communication* 35 (1985): 109–27.

Farris, Christine, and Chris M. Anson, eds. *Under Construction: Working at the Intersections of Composition Theory, Research, and Practice*. Logan: U of Utah P, 1998.

Fisher, Walter R. "Clarifying the Narrative Paradigm." *Communication Monographs* 56 (1989): 55–58.

———. "Narration as a Human Communication Paradigm: The Case of Public Moral Argument." *Contemporary Rhetorical Theory*. Ed. John Louis Lucaites, Celeste Michelle Condit, Sally Caudill. New York: Guilford, 1999. 265–87.

———. "Narration, Knowledge, and the Possibility of Wisdom." *Rethinking Knowledge: Reflections Across the Disciplines*. Ed. Robert F. Goodman and Walter R. Fisher. Albany: State U of New York P, 1995. 169–92.

———. "Toward a Logic of Good Reasons." *Quarterly Journal of Speech* 64 (1978): 376–84.

Fletcher, Angus. "Volume and Body in Burke's Criticism, or Stalled in the Right Place." *Representing Kenneth Burke: Selected Papers from the English Institute*. Ed. Hayden White and Margaret Brose. Baltimore: Johns Hopkins UP, 1982. 150–75.

Flores, Richard. Comment in "Forum: Problems with Personal Criticism." *PMLA* 111 (Oct. 1996): 1165–66.

Flynn, Elizabeth A. "Composing as a Woman." *CCC* 39 (1988): 423–35.

Fontaine, Sheryl I., and Susan Hunter, eds. *Writing Ourselves into the Story: Unheard Voices from Composition Studies*. Carbondale: Southern Illinois UP, 1993.

Ford, Marjorie, Jon Ford, and Ann Watters, eds. *Coming from Home: Readings for Writers*. New York: McGraw, 1993.

Foss, Sonja K., and Cindy L. Griffin. "Beyond Persuasion: A Proposal for an Invitational Rhetoric. *Communication Monographs* 62 (1995): 2–17.

France, Alan. "Dialectics of Self: Structure and Agency as the Subject of English." *College English* 63 (2000): 145–65.

Fraser, Nancy. "Rethinking the Public Sphere: A Contribution to the Critique of Actually Existing Democracy." *The Phantom Public Sphere*. Ed. Bruce Robbins. Minneapolis: U of Minnesota P, 1993. 1–32.

Frey, Olivia. "Beyond Literary Darwinism: Women's Voices and Critical Discourse. *College English* 52 (1990): 507–26.

Fulkerson, Richard. "Transcending Our Conception of Argument in Light of Feminist Critiques." *Argument and Advocacy* 32 (1996): 199–217.

Gage, John T. "An Adequate Epistemology for Composition: Classical and Modern Perspectives." Connors, Ede, and Lunsford 152–69.

Gale, Xin Lu. "Historical Studies and Postmodernism: Rereading Aspasia of Miletus." *College English* 62 (2000): 361–86.

Gere, Anne Ruggles. "Revealing Silence: Rethinking Personal Writing." *CCC* 53 (2001): 203–23.

Gilbert, G. Nigel, and Michael Mulkay. *Opening Pandora's Box: A Sociological Analysis of Scientists' Discourse*. Cambridge: Cambridge UP, 1984.

Gilligan, Carol. *In a Different Voice: Psychological Theory and Women's Development.* Cambridge: Harvard UP, 1982.

Gillmore, Leigh. *Autobiographics: A Feminist Theory of Women's Self-Representation.* Ithaca: Cornell UP, 1994.

Glenn, Cheryl. "Comment: Truth, Lies, and Method: Revisiting Feminist Historiography." *College English* 62 (2000): 387–89.

Griffin, C. W. "A Theory of Responding to Student Writing: The State of the Art." *CCC* 33 (1982): 296–301.

Grimaldi, William M. A. *Studies in the Philosophy of Aristotle's Rhetoric.* Weisbaden: Franz Steiner Verlag, 1972.

Grobman, Laurie. "'Just Multiculturalism': Teaching Writing as Critical and Ethical Practice." *JAC* 22 (2002): 815–45.

———. "(Re)Writing Youth: Basic Writing, Youth Culture, and Social Change." *Journal of Basic Writing* 20 (2001): 3–24.

Haefner, Joel. "Democracy, Pedagogy, and the Personal Essay." *College English* 54 (1992): 127–37.

Halloran, S. Michael. "Rhetoric in the American College Curriculum: The Decline of Public Discourse." *PRE/TEXT* 3 (1982): 245–69.

Hardison, O. B., Jr. "Binding Proteus: An Essay on the Essay." Butrym 11–28.

Harpham, Geoffrey Galt. "Ethics." *Critical Terms for Literary Study.* 2nd ed. Ed. Frank Lentricchia and Thomas McLaughlin. Chicago: U of Chicago P, 1995. 387–405.

Harris, Joseph. *A Teaching Subject: Composition since 1966.* Upper Saddle River: Prentice, 1997.

———. "The Idea of Community in the Study of Writing." *CCC* 40 (1989): 11–22.

———. "Person, Position, Style." Olson and Taylor 47–56.

Harris, Wendell V. "Reflections on the Peculiar Status of the Personal Essay." *College English* 58 (1996): 934–53.

Hauser, Gerard A. "Aristotle's Example Revisited." *Philosophy and Rhetoric* 18 (1985): 171–80.

Heilker, Paul. *The Essay: Theory and Pedagogy for an Active Form.* Urbana: NCTE, 1996.

Herrington, Anne. "When Is My Business Your Business?" in "The Politics of the Personal: Storying Our Lives Against the Grain." *College English* 64 (2001): 47–49.

Herzberg, Bruce. "Community Service and Critical Teaching." *CCC* 45 (1994): 307–19.

Hesse, Douglas. "A Boundary Zone: First-Person Short Stories and Narrative Essays." *Short Story Theory at a Crossroads.* Ed. Susan Lohafer and Jo Ellyn Clarey. Baton Rouge: Louisiana State UP, 1989. 85–105.

———. "Essay Form and *Auskomponierung*." Butrym 289–306.

———. "Essays and Experience, Time and Rhetoric." Clifford and Schilb 195–211.

———. "Stories in Essays, Essays as Stories." C. Anderson, *Literary* 176–96.

Herzberg, Bruce. "Community Service and Critical Teaching." *Writing in the Community: Concepts and Models for Service-Learning in Composition.* Ed. Linda Adler-Kassner, Robert Crooks, and Ann Watters. Washington: AAHE and NCTE, 1997. 57–69.

Hillocks, George, Jr. *Research on Written Composition: New Directions for Teaching.* Urbana: NCTE, 1986.

Himmelfarb, Gertrude. *On Looking into the Abyss: Untimely Thoughts on Culture and Society.* New York: Vintage, 1995.

Hindman, Jane E., guest ed. "Introduction to Special Focus: Personal Writing." *College English* 64 (2001): 34–40.

Holdstein, Deborah H., and David Bleich, eds. "Introduction: Recognizing the Human in the Humanities." *Personal Effects: The Social Character of Scholarly Writing.* Logan: Utah State UP, 2001. 1–24.

Howard, Rebecca Moore. "The Citation Functions: The Literary Production of Power—Citation Practices among Authors and Students." *Kairos* 3.1 (Spring 1998). 16 Aug. 2002 <http://www.english.ttu.edu/kairos/3.1/coverweb/ipc/practcite.htm>.

Jameson, Fredric. *The Political Unconscious: Narrative as a Socially Symbolic Act.* Ithaca: Cornell UP, 1981.

Jarratt, Susan C. "Comment: Rhetoric and Feminism: Together Again." *College English* 62 (2000): 390–93.

———. "Introduction: As We Were Saying . . ." Jarratt and Worsham 1–18.

Jarratt, Susan C., and Lynn Worsham, eds. *Feminism and Composition Studies: In Other Words.* New York: MLA, 1998.

Johnson, Mark. *The Body in the Mind: The Bodily Basis of Meaning, Imagination, and Reason.* Chicago: U of Chicago P, 1987.

Johnson, Nan. "Ethos and the Aims of Rhetoric." Connors, Ede, and Lunsford 98–114.

Kamler, Barbara. *Relocating the Personal: A Critical Writing Pedagogy.* Albany: State U of New York P, 2001.

Kingsolver, Barbara. *High Tide in Tucson: Essays from Now or Never.* New York: Harper, 1995.

Kinneavy, James L. "*Kairos*: A Neglected Concept in Classical Rhetoric." *Rhetoric and Praxis: The Contribution of Classical Rhetoric to Practical Reason.* Ed. J. D. Moss. Washington: Catholic U of America P, 1986. 79–105.

———. "*Kairos* in Aristotle's *Rhetoric*." *Written Communication* 17 (July 2000): 432–43.

Kirsch, Gesa E., and Min-Zhan Lu. "Symposium Collective" in "The Politics of the Personal: Storying Our Lives Against the Grain." *College English* 64 (Sept. 2001): 41–62.

Kirsch, Gesa E., and Joy S. Ritchie. "Beyond the Personal: Theorizing a Politics of Location in Composition Research." *CCC* 46 (1995): 7–29.

Klaus, Carl H. "The Chameleon 'I': On Voice and Personality in the Personal Essay." *Voices on Voice: Perspectives, Definitions, Inquiry.* Ed. Kathleen Blake Yancey. Urbana: NCTE, 1994. 111–29.

———. "Essayists on the Essay." C. Anderson, *Literary* 155–75.

———. "Montaigne and His Essays: Toward a Poetics of the Self." *Iowa Review* 20 (1990): 1–23.

Kress, G. "Writing and Learning to Write." *The Handbook of Human Development.* Ed. D. R. Olsen and N. Torrance. London: Blackwell, 1996.

Laird, Ellen A. "Daisies." *TETYC* 26 (1998): 121–24.

Lamb, Catherine E. "Beyond Argument in Feminist Composition." *CCC* 42 (1991): 11–24.

Lanser, Susan Sniader. *The Narrative Act: Point of View in Prose Fiction.* Princeton: Princeton, 1981.

Latour, Bruno, and Stephen Woolgar. *Laboratory Life: The Social Construction of Scientific Facts.* Beverly Hills: Sage, 1979.

LeFevre, Karen Burke. *Invention as a Social Act.* Carbondale: Southern Illinois UP, 1987.

Leff, Michael. "The Habitation of Rhetoric." *Contemporary Rhetorical Theory: A Reader.* Ed. John Louis Lucaites, Celeste Michelle Condit, Sally Caudill. New York: Guilford, 1999. 52–64.

Lejeune, Philippe. *On Autobiography.* Ed. Paul John Eakin. Trans. Katherine Leary. Minneapolis: U of Minnesota P, 1989.

Lu, Min-Zhan. "Conflict and Struggle: The Enemies or Preconditions of Basic Writing?" *College English* 54 (1992): 887–913.

Lucaites, John L., and Celeste M. Condit. "Re-Constructing Narrative Theory: A Functional Perspective." *Journal of Communication* 35 (1985): 90–108.

Lunsford, Andrea A., and John J. Ruszkiewicz. *Everything's an Argument.* Boston: Bedford/St. Martin's, 1999.

Lunsford, Andrea A., and Lisa S. Ede. "On Distinctions between Classical and Modern Rhetoric." Connors, Ede, and Lunsford 37–50.

Lynch, Dennis A., Diana George, and Marilyn M. Cooper. "Moments of Argument: Agonistic Inquiry and Confrontational Cooperation." *CCC* 48 (1997): 61–85.

Lyotard, Jean-François. *The Postmodern Condition: A Report on Knowledge.* Trans. Geoff Bennington and Brian Massumi. Minneapolis: U of Minnesota P, 1989.

MacDonald, Susan Peck. "Voices of Research: Methodological Choices of a Disciplinary Community." Farris and Anson 111–23.

Mahala, Daniel, and Jody Swilky. "Telling Stories, Speaking Personally: Reconsidering the Place of Lived Experience in Composition." *JAC* 16 (1996): 363–88.

Martin, Wallace. *Recent Theories of Narrative.* Ithaca: Cornell UP, 1986.

McCarthy, Mary. *Memories of a Catholic Girlhood.* New York: Harcourt, 1957.

McGee, Michael C., and John S. Nelson. "Reason in Public Argument." *Journal of Communication* 35 (1985): 139–55.

McNabb, Richard. "Making the Gesture: Graduate Student Submissions and the Expectation of Journal Referees." *Composition Studies* 29 (Spring 2001): 9–26.

McQuade, Donald, and Robert Atwan, eds. *The Writer's Presence: A Pool of Readings.* 3rd ed. Boston: Bedford/St. Martin's, 2000.

Miller, Nancy K. *Getting Personal: Feminist Occasions and Other Autobiographical Acts.* New York: Routledge, 1991.

Miller, Richard E. "Fault Lines in the Contact Zone." *College English* 56 (1994): 389–408.

Miller, Susan. "Two Comments on 'A Common Ground: The Essay in Academe.'" *College English* 52 (1990): 330–34.

Molloy, Sylvia. "Mock Heroics and Personal Markings." *PMLA* 111 (Oct. 1996): 1072–75.

Morgan, Dan. "Opinion: Ethical Issues Raised by Students' Personal Writing." *College English* 60 (1998): 318–25.

Murray, Donald L. *A Writer Teaches Writing.* 2nd ed. Boston: Houghton, 1985.

Mutnick, Deborah. "Rethinking the Personal Narrative: Life-Writing and Composition Pedagogy." Farris and Anson 79–92.

Olney, James. *Metaphors of the Self: The Meaning of Autobiography.* Princeton: Princeton UP, 1972.

Olson, Gary A., and Todd W. Taylor, eds. *Publishing in Rhetoric and Composition.* Albany: State U of New York P, 1997.

Paley, Grace. *Enormous Changes at the Last Minute.* New York: Farrar, 1974.

Paley, Karen Surman. *I-Writing: The Politics and Practice of Teaching First-Person Writing.* Carbondale: Southern Illinois UP, 2001.

Raymond, James C. "Enthymemes, Examples, and Rhetorical Method." Connors, Ede, and Lunsford 140–51.

Rich, Adrienne. "When We Dead Awaken: Writing as Re-Vision." *College English* 34 (1972): 18–25.

———. "Notes on a Politics of Location (1984)." *Blood, Bread, and Poetry: Selected Prose, 1979–1985.* Adrienne Rich. New York: Norton, 1994. 210–31.

Ritchie, Joy, and Kathleen Boardman. "Feminism in Composition: Inclusion, Metonymy, and Disruption." *CCC* 50 (1999): 585–606.

Ritchie, Joy, and Kate Ronald. "Riding Long Coattails, Subverting Tradition: The Tricky Business of Feminists Teaching Rhetoric(s)." Jarratt and Worsham 217–38.

Rodriguez, Richard. *Hunger of Memory: The Education of Richard Rodriguez*. New York: Bantam, 1983.

Ronald, Kate. "A Reexamination of Personal and Public Discourse in Classical Rhetoric." *Rhetoric Review* 9 (1990): 36–48.

Rose, Mike. *Lives on the Boundary: The Struggles and Achievements of America's Underprepared*. New York: Free, 1989.

Rowland, Robert. "On Limiting the Narrative Paradigm: Three Case Studies." *Communication Monographs* 56 (1989): 39–54.

Sanders, Scott Russell. "The Singular First Person." Butrym 31–42.

Scott, Joan W. "The Evidence of Experience." *Critical Inquiry* 17 (1991): 773–97.

———. "Experience." *Feminists Theorize the Political*. Ed. Judith Butler and Joan W. Scott. New York: Routledge, 1992. 22–40.

———. "A Rejoinder to Thomas C. Holt." *Questions of Evidence: Proof, Practice, and Persuasion Across the Disciplines*. Ed. James Chandler, Arnold I. Davidson, and Harry Harootunian. Chicago: U of Chicago P, 1994. 397–400.

Smith, Paul. *Discerning the Subject*. Minneapolis: Minnesota UP, 1988.

Smith, Sidonie, and Julia Watson. *Reading Autobiography: A Guide for Interpreting Life Narratives*. Minneapolis: U of Minnesota P, 2001.

Sommers, Nancy. "Between the Drafts." *CCC* 43 (1992): 23–31.

———. "Responding to Student Writing." *CCC* 33 (1982): 148–56.

Spellmeyer, Kurt. "A Common Ground: The Essay in the Academy." *College English* 51 (1989): 262–76.

Stewart, Donald. "Collaborative Learning and Composition: Boon or Bane?" *Rhetoric Review* 7 (1988): 58–83.

Straub, Richard. "Students' Reactions to Teacher Comments: An Exploratory Study." *Research in the Teaching of English* 31 (1997): 91–119.

Sukenick, Lynn. "On Women and Fiction." *The Authority of Experience: Essays in Feminist Criticism*. Ed. Arlyn Diamond and Lee R. Edwards. Amherst: U of Massachusetts P, 1977. 28–44.

Sullivan, Dale L. "The Ethos of Epideictic Encounter." *Philosophy and Rhetoric* 26 (1993): 113–33.

Summerfield, Judith. "Is There a Life in This Text? Reimagining Narrative." Clifford and Schilb 179–94.

Tompkins, Jane. "Me and My Shadow." *New Literary History* 19 (1987): 169–78.

Trimbur, John. "Consensus and Difference in Collaborative Learning." *College English* 51 (1989): 602–16.

Trimmer, Joseph F. "Narration as Knowledge." NCTE Conference on Stories in the Classroom. Tucson, Apr. 1999.

———. *Narration as Knowledge: Tales of the Teaching Life.* Portsmouth: Boynton/Cook, 1997.

van Peer, Willie, and Seymour Chatman, eds. "Introduction." *New Perspectives on Narrative Perspective.* Albany: State U of New York P, 2001. 1–17.

Villanueva, Victor, Jr. *Bootstraps: From an American Academic of Color.* Urbana: NCTE, 1993.

———. "The Personal" in "The Politics of the Personal: Storying Our Lives Against the Grain." *College English* 64 (Sept. 2001): 50–52.

Walker, Alice. "Beauty: When the Other Dancer Is the Self." *In Search* 361–70.

———. "Beyond the Peacock: The Reconstruction of Flannery O'Connor." *In Search* 42–59.

———. "In Search of Our Mothers' Gardens." *In Search* 231–43.

———. *In Search of Our Mothers' Gardens.* San Diego: Harcourt, 1983.

Walker, Jeffrey. "*Pathos* and *Katharis* in 'Aristotelian' Rhetoric: Some Implications." *Rereading Aristotle's* Rhetoric. Ed. Alan G. Gross and Arthur E. Walzer. Carbondale: Southern Illinois UP, 2000. 74–92.

Ward, Irene. "How Democratic Can We Get? The Internet, the Public Sphere, and Public Discourse." *JAC* 17 (1997): 365–79.

Weisser, Christian R. *Moving Beyond Academic Discourse: Composition Studies and the Public Sphere.* Carbondale: Southern Illinois UP, 2002.

Wells, Susan. "The Doubleness of Writing and Permission to Lie." Clifford and Schilb 109–23.

———. "Rogue Cops and Health Care: What Do We Want from Public Writing?" *CCC* 47 (1996): 325–41.

White, E. B. "Foreword." *Essays of E. B. White.* New York: Harper, 1977. vii–ix.

———. "Sootfall and Fallout." *Essays of E. B. White.* New York: Harper, 1977. 90–99.

White, Hayden. *Metahistory: The Historical Imagination in Nineteenth-Century Europe.* Baltimore: Johns Hopkins UP, 1973.

Williams, Bronwyn T. "Never Let the Truth Stand in the Way of a Good Story: A Work for Three Voices." *College English* 65 (2003): 290–304.

Williams, Patricia J. *The Alchemy of Race and Rights.* Cambridge: Harvard UP, 1991.

Woolf, Virginia. *A Room of One's Own.* New York: Harcourt, 1957.

Worsham, Lynn. "After Words: A Choice of Words Remains." Jarratt and Worsham 329–56.

———. "Coming to Terms: Theory, Writing, Politics." *Rhetoric and Composition as Intellectual Work.* Ed. Gary A. Olson. Carbondale: Southern Illinois UP, 2002. 101–14.

Yancey, Kathleen Blake. "On Feminist Research: What Do Women Want (Now)?, or A Query Regarding Con/Textual Relationships." *Feminist Empirical Research: Emerging Perspectives on Qualitative and Teacher Research*. Ed. Joanne Addison and Sharon James McGee. Portsmouth: Boynton/Cook, 1999. 145–57.

Zak, Frances, and Christopher C. Weaver, eds. *The Theory and Practice of Grading Writing: Problems and Possibilities*. Albany: State U of New York P, 1998.

Zeiger, William. "The Exploratory Essay: Enfranchising the Spirit of Inquiry in College Composition." *College English* 47 (1985): 454–66.

Zinsser, William. "Introduction." *Inventing the Truth: The Art and Craft of Memoir*. 2nd ed. Ed. William Zinsser. Boston: Houghton, 1995. 3–20.

Index

abstract discourse, 26
academic discourse: alternatives to, 64–66; argument in, 8–12; blended with personal writing, 2–3; communities, 7; personal evidence as supplement for, 93–94; scope of, 6–8
"After Words: A Choice of Words Remains" (Worsham), 11, 15–21
Alchemy of Race and Rights, The (Williams), 5
alternative discourses, 35, 37, 64–66, 114
analysis, 95, 147n. 9
Anderson, Chris, 146n. 7, 152–53n. 15
Anson, Chris, 105
anti-identification, 18–19, 148n. 12
appropriateness, academic, 17–22, 148n. 15
argument, xv, 7, 56, 90; in academic discourse, 8–12; in classical tradition, 84–87; collegial, 9–10, 146nn. 6, 7; enthymemes, 86, 88, 124; feminist perspective on, 11–12, 146n. 6; inductive, 102, 157nn. 5, 6. *See also* personal academic argument
argument-narrative dichotomy, 8–9
"Aria" (Rodriguez), 117–18
Aristotle, 19–20, 42, 56, 61–62, 84–87, 156n. 1
assumptions, interrogation of, 100–104
Atwan, Robert, 111

audience, 42, 72, 79; anti-identification and, 18–19, 148n. 12; assumptions of, 100–102; classical tradition and, 45, 85–86, 88, 100, 102, 150–51n. 8; enthymemes and, 86, 88; identification and, 19, 51–53; persona constructed for, 47–48; politics of location and, 35–38
authenticity, 61, 66, 125–26
author, real and implied, 40, 150n. 7
autobiographical pact, 67, 73, 129, 154n. 6
autobiography, 17; and ethics of disclosure, 94–95; fabrications in, 67, 73, 75, 128–29, 159–60n. 3; fictional elements, 66–72; memory and, 66–69; as socially constructed, 75–76, 154n. 7
autoethnography, 4–5

Bakhtin, Mikhail, 48
Bal, Miecke, 150n. 7
Ballenger, Bruce, 129
Barthes, Roland, 41
Bartholomae, David, 23, 150n. 5
Bean, Janet, 80
"Beauty: When the Other Dancer Is the Self" (Walker), 4
"Beginning Adult Women Students as College Writers" (Lindgren), 79–80
Behar, Ruth, 155–56n. 12
Belenky, Mary Field, 11–12
Berlin, James, 13, 23–24

rhetorical personal, in student writing, 54–57
Rich, Adrienne, 34, 149n. 1
Ritchie, Joy S., 11, 13, 33–34, 76
Rodriguez, Richard, 4, 21–22, 117–18
Roland Barthes by Roland Barthes (Barthes), 41
Ronald, Kate, 33–34, 85
Room of One's Own, A (Woolf), 41
Ruszkiewicz, John J., 10

Sanders, Scott Russell, 40–41, 72–73
Sartre, Jean-Paul, 59–60
scholarly writing, 8
scientific orientation, 90, 114
Scott, Joan W., 64, 76, 92–93, 149n. 19, 154n. 4, 158.n 11
self, 38, 154n. 7. *See also* subject
sentimentality, 18
service-learning, 131–32
silenced voices, 18, 24
"Skunk Dreams" (Erdrich), 1–2, 54
Smith, Paul, 149n. 2
Smith, Sidonie, 73, 85, 145n. 1
social, the, versus the personal, 30
Sommers, Nancy, 12
sources: in academic essays, 120–25; demystification of, 120–22; student engagement with, 115–20
Spellmeyer, Kurt, 59–60, 117
Stewart, Donald, 23
student writers: demystification of sources, 120–22; development of, through writing, 91–92; subject formation and, 13, 25, 30; subject position taken by, 77–78
student writing: construction of subject in, 45–49, 125–30; disclosure in, 17, 21, 66, 96–97, 113; divergence from assigned readings in, 54–60, 121–22; evaluation of text versus life in, 96–97,

129–30, 155n. 9; experience as fiction in, 66–72; fabrications in, 128–29, 159–60n. 3; orientations in, 91–92, 124–25; revision in, 99, 103, 112; rhetorical personal in, 54–57; supplement and surplus in, 104–5, 124. *See also* personal writing; writing instruction
subject, 149n. 2; character and, 42–44; construct of personal, 38–45; fragmented, 39–41, 50–51; implied author as, 40, 150n. 7; multiple positions of, 38–39, 48, 52–53; narrative, 69–70; postmodern view of, 24–25, 31, 38–45; in student writing, 45–49, 125–30; transformation of, through writing, 48–49. *See also* narrator
subject formation, 13, 25, 30
subjectivity, as discursive event, 92–93
"Subverting Ideologies and Understanding Racism" (student es say), 45–49
Sukenick, Lynn, 32, 33
Summerfield, Judith, 63, 110–11, 126, 130, 155n. 9
supplement, 93, 124, 135; of personal narrative, 104–7
surplus, 3, 83–84, 92–95, 135; instruction methods and, 107–8; in student writing, 104–5, 124

Tarule, Jill Mattuck, 11–12
teaching. *See* writing instruction
"Teaching College English as a Woman" (Bloom), 12
Teaching English in the Two-Year College, 13
"Television and Family Rituals" (Winn), 120–21

CANDACE SPIGELMAN is an associate professor at Penn State Berks–Lehigh Valley College, where she serves as co-coordinator of professional writing and teaches composition, rhetorical theory, English language analysis, and peer tutoring in writing. Her publications include *Across Property Lines: Textual Ownership in Writing Groups; On Location: Theory and Practice in Classroom-Based Writing Tutoring* (forthcoming); and articles in *College English, CCC, JAC,* and *Composition Studies.* She received the 2002 Richard Ohmann Award for her article "Argument and Evidence in the Case of the Personal."

 *Studies in Writing & Rhetoric*

In 1980 the Conference on College Composition and Communication established the Studies in Writing & Rhetoric (SWR) series as a forum for monograph-length arguments or presentations that engage general compositionists. SWR encourages extended essays or research reports addressing any issue in composition and rhetoric from any theoretical or research perspective as long as the general significance to the field is clear. Previous SWR publications serve as models for prospective authors; in addition, contributors may propose alternate formats and agendas that inform or extend the field's current debates.

SWR is particularly interested in projects that connect the specific research site or theoretical framework to contemporary classroom and institutional contexts of direct concern to compositionists across the nation. Such connections may come from several approaches, including cultural, theoretical, field-based, gendered, historical, and interdisciplinary. SWR especially encourages monographs by scholars early in their careers, by established scholars who wish to share an insight or exhortation with the field, and by scholars of color.

The SWR series editor and editorial board members are committed to working closely with prospective authors and offering significant developmental advice for encouraged manuscripts and prospectuses. Editorships rotate every five years. Prospective authors intending to submit a prospectus during the 2002 to 2007 editorial appointment should obtain submission guidelines from Robert Brooke, SWR editor, University of Nebraska–Lincoln, Department of English, P.O. Box 880337, 202 Andrews Hall, Lincoln, NE 68588-0337.

General inquiries may also be addressed to Sponsoring Editor, Studies in Writing & Rhetoric, Southern Illinois University Press, P.O. Box 3697, Carbondale, IL 62902-3697.